Super Easy
CROCK POT
COOKBOOK
for Beginners

Miayualia Mikujakelsen

1900 Days Quick & Mouthwatering Slow Cooker Recipes Book with Step-by-Step Instructions | No-Stress 30-Day Meal Plan

Warning-Disclaimer

The purpose of this book is to educate and entertain. The author or publisher does not guarantee that anyone following the techniques, suggestions, tips, ideas, or strategies will become successful. The author and publisher shall have neither liability or responsibility to anyone with respect to any loss or damage caused, or alleged to be caused, directly or indirectly by the information contained in this book.

TABLE OF CONTENTS

INTRODUCTION

In today's fast-paced world, finding the time to prepare healthy, delicious meals can feel like a challenge. Between balancing work, family, and personal time, cooking often gets pushed to the back burner. That's where the *Crock Pot* comes in—a revolutionary kitchen appliance that brings slow cooking to the forefront of meal preparation. With the Crock Pot, you can prepare hearty, flavorful meals with minimal effort, allowing you to enjoy more time with family or focus on other priorities while your meal slowly simmers to perfection.

This cookbook is your ultimate guide to mastering the art of Crock Pot cooking. Whether you're a seasoned slow-cooker enthusiast or someone new to the concept, this book will provide you with all the tools and inspiration you need to create flavorful, nutritious meals that fit seamlessly into your busy lifestyle.

The Benefits of Slow Cooking

The beauty of Crock Pot cooking lies in its simplicity. At its core, the Crock Pot allows you to set it and forget it, turning raw ingredients into rich, mouth-watering dishes with minimal supervision. But beyond convenience, slow cooking offers a range of benefits that make it an indispensable tool for today's home cook.

1. Time-Saving Convenience: The Crock Pot is ideal for people with hectic schedules. With a little bit of prep work in the morning or the night before, you can come home to a fully cooked meal that's ready to serve. Whether you're juggling work, school, or other responsibilities, the slow cooker allows you to plan your meals ahead, freeing up time during your busiest hours.

2. Enhanced Flavor Development: One of the standout qualities of slow cooking is its ability to develop deep, complex flavors. As food cooks slowly over several hours, the ingredients meld together, resulting in rich, layered tastes that are difficult to achieve with other cooking methods. Meats become more tender, sauces become more infused with flavor, and spices have time to release their full potential.

3. Nutrient Retention: Slow cooking is also a healthier way to prepare food. Unlike some high-heat methods that can degrade certain nutrients, slow cooking helps retain more vitamins and minerals in your meals. This gentle cooking method allows you to create nutrient-dense dishes packed with vegetables, lean proteins, and whole grains, without compromising on flavor or texture.

4. Budget-Friendly Meals: The Crock Pot is a fantastic tool for creating budget-conscious meals. Slow cooking makes even tougher cuts of meat tender and flavorful, allowing you to get the most out of affordable ingredients. By using beans, grains, and seasonal vegetables, you can also reduce your grocery bill while still preparing wholesome and filling meals for the entire family.

5. Less Stress, More Satisfaction: There's something undeniably satisfying about walking into your home after a long day and being greeted by the aroma of a home-cooked meal. The stress of dinnertime disappears when you know your Crock Pot has been working all day to prepare something delicious for you and your loved ones. Whether it's a comforting soup, a savory stew, or a tender roast, slow-cooked meals bring warmth and ease to your dinner table.

Why the Crock Pot Stands Out

There are many kitchen gadgets available today, but the Crock Pot remains a favorite for home cooks of all skill levels—and with good reason. Its simplicity, versatility, and efficiency make it an invaluable tool in the modern kitchen.

♦ **- Set It and Forget It:** One of the most appealing aspects of the Crock Pot is its hands-off cooking process. Once you've prepped your ingredients and set the timer, the Crock Pot does the rest of the work. You don't need to constantly check on your meal or worry about burning food. This allows you to carry on with your day, whether that means working, running errands, or simply relaxing at home.

♦ **Versatility:** The Crock Pot is capable of cooking a wide range of dishes. From soups and stews to casseroles, roasts, and even desserts, there's no limit to what you can create in your slow cooker. It's a versatile tool that adapts to various cuisines and dietary preferences, making it a go-to for nearly any meal.

♦ **Energy Efficiency:** Slow cooking uses less energy compared to traditional ovens and stovetops. This makes it an environmentally friendly choice for those looking to reduce their energy consumption. Additionally, the Crock Pot's low energy use can help lower your household utility costs over time.

♦ **Batch Cooking and Meal Prep:** The Crock Pot is perfect for those who like to meal prep or cook in batches. Because it allows you to cook large quantities of food at once, you can easily prepare enough to enjoy throughout the week or freeze for later. This is especially helpful for families or individuals who want to maintain a healthy diet but don't have time to cook every day.

The Art of Slow Cooking

At its core, Crock Pot cooking is about embracing the slow, steady process of preparing food. It's a reminder that good things take time—and the results are worth the wait. However, there are a few tips and techniques that can help you get the most out of your Crock Pot and elevate your meals to the next level:

1. Layering Ingredients: When using a Crock Pot, the way you layer your ingredients can make a big difference in how your meal turns out. Denser vegetables like potatoes and carrots should be placed at the bottom of the pot, where they'll receive more heat. Softer vegetables and meats can be placed on top to ensure even cooking.

2. Don't Overfill the Pot: While it might be tempting to pack as much food as possible into your Crock Pot, it's important not to overfill it. Overloading the Crock Pot can lead to uneven cooking and may prevent your meal from reaching the right temperature. As a general rule, the pot should be filled no more than two-thirds full for the best results.

3. Browning Meat for Extra Flavor: Although it's not always necessary, browning meat before adding it to the Crock Pot can enhance the flavor of your dish. Searing the meat on the stovetop helps develop a caramelized crust, adding depth to stews, roasts, and chili.

4. Timing Is Key: Most Crock Pot recipes offer flexibility in cooking times, often allowing you to cook on either a low or high setting. Cooking on low heat for a longer period of time usually yields the best results, especially for tougher cuts of meat. However, if you're short on time, the high setting can be a good option for quicker meals.

5. Keep the Lid On: One of the golden rules of Crock Pot cooking is to resist the urge to lift the lid while your meal is cooking. Each time you remove the lid, valuable heat escapes, which can extend the cooking time and affect the final result. Trust the process and let the Crock Pot do its job without frequent interruptions.

A Return to Comfort and Connection

In a world where speed and efficiency often take precedence, the Crock Pot invites us to slow down and enjoy the process of cooking and eating. It allows us to create meals that are not only delicious but also comforting and nourishing. Whether you're cooking for yourself, your family, or a gathering of friends, the Crock Pot brings people together around the table, making mealtime more meaningful and less stressful.

The Crock Pot Cookbook is your guide to creating flavorful, nutritious meals with ease. Through the power of slow cooking, you can embrace a more relaxed and enjoyable approach to meal preparation, knowing that your Crock Pot will help you create something truly special. Let this cookbook inspire you to discover the joys of slow cooking and enjoy the warmth, flavor, and satisfaction it brings into your kitchen.

30-Day Meal Plan

DAYS	BREAKFAST	LUNCH	DINNER	SNACK/DESSERT
1	Coconut Protein Loaf 10	Smoky Baked Bean Casserole 19	Salmon with Lime Juice 47	Healthy Cinnamon Apple Delight 87
2	Spanakopita Frittata 8	Risotto alla Milanese 19	Slow-Cooked Pork Chops with Green Beans 38	Cherry Cobbler 88
3	Slow-Cooked Apple Cinnamon Oatmeal 8	Hearty Quinoa Chicken Chili 22	Provencal Poached Salmon with Herb Cream Sauce 51	Decadent Hot Fudge Cake 87
4	Croque Monsieur Strata 8	Scandinavian-Style Sweet and Savory Beans 19	Hearty Mulligan Chicken Stew 30	Maple Pumpkin Bread Pudding Delight 90
5	Slow-Cooked Bacon and Egg Breakfast Bake 8	Risotto with Gorgonzola 22	Mediterranean Cod Gratin with Three Cheeses 49	Peanut Butter Chocolate Delight Cake 89
6	Granola 10	Crock Pot Kidney Beans 20	Jerk Chicken 30	Piña Colada Bread Pudding 88
7	Cheesy Broccoli and Egg Casserole 10	Sweet and Tangy Mixed Bean Medley 20	Orange-Spiced Chicken with Sweet Potatoes 26	Blueberry Crisp 93
8	Nutty Oatmeal 12	White Beans with Kale 20	Barbecued Brisket 42	Ginger-Spiced Pumpkin Pudding 89
9	Toasted Maple Nut Granola 10	Earthy Whole Brown Lentil Dhal 19	Cajun Shrimp and Andouille Sausage Stew 51	Rum Raisin Arborio Pudding 88
10	Banana Bread Casserole 13	Cornbread-Topped Chili Beans 20	Hearty Italian Chicken and Bean Stew 33	Caramel Apples 92
11	Overnight Blueberry Cream Cheese French Toast 10	Cheesy Broccoli Rice Bake 23	Thai Peanut Wings 32	Crock-Baked Apples 90
12	Welsh Rarebit 13	Spicy Black Beans with Root Veggies 23	Creamy Chicken Curry 28	Maple Cinnamon Crème Brûlée 88
13	Slow-Cooked Mixed Fruit Compote 13	Creamy Butternut Squash Risotto 21	Barbecued Turkey 28	Decadent Double Chocolate Bread Pudding 91
14	Peach French Toast Bake 11	Barbecued Lima Beans 21	Chicken and Sausage Cacciatore 27	Crunchy Peanut Butter Candy Clusters 92
15	Slow-Cooked Cinnamon Rolls with Lemon Glaze 11	Savory Farro and Mushroom Pilaf 21	Spicy Tomato Basil Mussels 49	Port-Infused Figs with Blue Cheese 91
16	Breakfast Oatmeal 11	Apple-Cranberry Multigrain Hot Cereal 21	Mediterranean-Style Slow-Cooked Spareribs 41	Cardamom-Infused Pakistani Sweet Rice 92

DAYS	BREAKFAST	LUNCH	DINNER	SNACK/DESSERT
17	Slow-Cooked Maple Oatmeal Bake 11	Slow-Cooked Herb-Infused Rice 21	Spicy Taco Beef Stew 37	Sour-Cream Cheesecake 86
18	Vegetable Omelet 12	Cheesy Grits Casserole 23	Pacifica Sweet-Hot Salmon 49	Cinnamon-Spiced Stuffed Apples 90
19	Crockpot Asparagus and Bacon Frittata 16	Slow-Cooked Duck Confit 25	Ginger-Soy Pacific Chicken Thighs 34	Decadent Crock Pot Chocolate Clusters 73
20	Basic Strata 9	Pesto Chicken with Rustic Stewed Vegetables 26	Creamy Tarragon Chicken Delight 30	Peach-Pecan Grunt 87
21	Cheesy Vegetable and Ham Strata 9	Dad's Hearty Spicy Chicken Curry 27	Barbecued Chicken Legs 31	Sweet and Spicy Mustard Dogs 70
22	Streusel Cake 9	Zesty Garlic-Lime Chicken 29	Lemon Garlic Butter Halibut 48	Brownies with Nuts 86
23	Overnight Apple Cinnamon Oatmeal 9	Marinated Chinese Chicken Salad 29	Braised Lamb Shanks with Olives and Potatoes 45	Apple-Pear Streusel 92
24	Slow-Cooked Fruited Oatmeal with Nuts 16	Tomato Chicken Curry 32	Sweet and Spicy Hawaiian Sausages 44	Zesty Spicy Nut Medley 72
25	Crock Pot Zucchini-Carrot Bread 17	Boneless Buffalo Chicken for Sandwiches 25	Garlic-Infused Veal Stew 40	Cheesy Italian Tomato Fondue 68
26	Pumpkin-Pecan N'Oatmeal 15	Slow-Cooked Chicken Jambalaya 25	Spicy Seafood Laksa 52	Tropical Coconut Macadamia Bread Pudding 90
27	Crock Pot Egg-Potato Bake 12	Bacon-Mushroom Chicken 28	Lamb Shanks and Potatoes 44	Butterscotch Haystacks 74
28	Carrot Cake Oatmeal 12	Chicken Chili Verde 26	Mariner's Delight Shellfish Stew 65	Maple-Sage Sweet Potatoes with Apples 83
29	Slow-Cooker Enchiladas Verde 17	Pizza Rice 22	Sea Bass Tagine 50	Pineapple Sweet Potatoes 80
30	Crock Pot Frittata Provencal 15	Quick and Simple Baked Beans 20	Mahi-Mahi with Tropical Salsa and Orange Lentils 50	Sweet and Spicy Peanuts 68

Chapter 1

Breakfasts

Chapter 1 Breakfasts

Slow-Cooked Apple Cinnamon Oatmeal

Prep time: 10 minutes | Cook time: 6 to 8 hours | Serves 4

- 2 cups skim or 2% milk
- 2 tablespoons honey, or ¼ cup brown sugar
- 1 tablespoon margarine
- ¼ teaspoon salt
- ½ teaspoon ground

- cinnamon
- 1 cup dry rolled oats
- 1 cup apples, chopped
- ½ cup raisins (optional)
- ¼ cup walnuts, chopped
- ½ cup fat-free half-and-half

1. Spray inside of crock pot with nonfat cooking spray. 2. In a mixing bowl, combine all ingredients except half-and-half. Pour into cooker. 3. Cover and cook on low overnight, ideally 6 to 8 hours. The oatmeal is ready to eat in the morning. 4. Stir in the half-and-half just before serving.

Croque Monsieur Strata

Prep time: 10 minutes | Cook time: 4½ hours | Serves 8

- 8 large eggs
- 2 cups whole or low-fat milk
- 6 shakes Tabasco sauce
- 1 tablespoon Dijon mustard
- 8 cups torn soft-crusted French bread (if the crust is crispy, remove it and use

- the center of the bread)
- 8 ounces (227 g) sliced Black Forest ham, cut into matchsticks
- 3 cups shredded Gruyère cheese
- 4 tablespoons (½ stick) unsalted butter, melted

1. Begin by coating the insert of a 5- to 7-quart crock pot with nonstick cooking spray or lining it with a slow-cooker liner according to the manufacturer's instructions. 2. In a large bowl, whisk together the eggs, milk, Tabasco sauce, and mustard until well combined. Then, add the bread and diced ham, stirring to ensure the bread is fully saturated and the ham is evenly distributed. 3. Spoon half of the bread and ham mixture into the crock pot, then sprinkle half of the cheese on top. Repeat this layering process and finish with a drizzle of melted butter. 4. Cover the crock pot and cook on low for 4 hours, or until the strata reaches an internal temperature of 170°F (77°C) on an instant-read thermometer.

Afterward, remove the lid and cook for an additional 30 minutes to finish. 5. Once cooked, serve the strata directly from the crock pot, keeping it set on warm to maintain temperature.

Slow-Cooked Bacon and Egg Breakfast Bake

Prep time: 15 minutes | Cook time: 5 to 6 hours | Serves 8

- 1 tablespoon bacon fat or extra-virgin olive oil
- 12 eggs
- 1 cup coconut milk
- 1 pound (454 g) bacon, chopped and cooked crisp

- ½ sweet onion, chopped
- 2 teaspoons minced garlic
- ¼ teaspoon freshly ground black pepper
- ⅛ teaspoon salt
- Pinch red pepper flakes

1. Lightly grease the insert of the crock pot with the bacon fat or olive oil. 2. In a medium bowl, whisk together the eggs, coconut milk, bacon, onion, garlic, pepper, salt, and red pepper flakes. Pour the mixture into the crock pot. 3. Cover and cook on low for 5 to 6 hours. 4. Serve warm.

Spanakopita Frittata

Prep time: 10 minutes | Cook time: 5 to 6 hours | Serves 8

- 1 tablespoon extra-virgin olive oil
- 12 eggs
- 1 cup heavy (whipping) cream
- 2 teaspoons minced garlic
- 2 cups chopped spinach

- ½ cup feta cheese
- Cherry tomatoes, halved, for garnish (optional)
- Yogurt, for garnish (optional)
- Parsley, for garnish (optional)

1. Begin by lightly greasing the insert of the crock pot with olive oil. 2. In a medium bowl, whisk together the eggs, heavy cream, garlic, spinach, and feta cheese until well combined. Pour this mixture into the greased crock pot. 3. Cover the crock pot and cook on low for 5 to 6 hours until set. 4. When serving, top the dish with fresh tomatoes, a dollop of yogurt, and a sprinkle of parsley, if desired.

Basic Strata

- 8 cups torn or cubed (1-inch) stale bread, tough crusts removed
- 3½ to 4 cups shredded cheese
- 10 large eggs
- 3 cups milk
- 1½ teaspoons salt
- ½ teaspoon hot sauce

1. Begin by coating the insert of a 5- to 7-quart crock pot with nonstick cooking spray or lining it with a slow-cooker liner according to the manufacturer's instructions. 2. Spread a layer of bread in the bottom of the crock pot and sprinkle with some of the cheese. Continue layering the bread and cheese until all ingredients are used, reserving some cheese for the top layer. 3. In a large bowl, whisk together the eggs, milk, salt, and hot sauce until well combined. Pour this mixture over the layered bread and cheese, pressing down gently to ensure the bread absorbs the liquid. Sprinkle the reserved cheese on top. 4. Cover the crock pot and cook on low for 4 hours, or until the strata is fully cooked and reaches an internal temperature of 170°F (77°C) when checked with an instant-read thermometer. After this time, remove the lid and cook for an additional 30 minutes to firm up the dish. 5. Once done, serve the strata directly from the crock pot, keeping it set on warm for your guests to enjoy.

Cheesy Vegetable and Ham Strata

- 1 tablespoon extra-virgin olive oil
- 1 tablespoon butter
- 1 onion, chopped
- 2 garlic cloves, minced
- 1½ cups baby spinach leaves
- 1 red bell pepper, chopped
- 1 large tomato, seeded and chopped
- 1 cup cubed ham
- Nonstick cooking spray
- 5 eggs, beaten
- 1 cup milk
- ½ teaspoon salt
- ½ teaspoon dried thyme leaves
- ⅛ teaspoon freshly ground black pepper
- 6 slices French bread, cubed
- 1 cup shredded Cheddar cheese
- ½ cup shredded Swiss cheese
- ¼ cup grated Parmesan cheese

1. In a medium saucepan over medium heat, heat the olive oil and butter. Add the onion and garlic, and sauté, stirring, until tender, about 6 minutes. 2. Add the spinach and cook until wilted, about 5 minutes. Remove from the heat and add the bell pepper, tomato, and ham. 3. Line the crock pot with heavy-duty foil and spray with the nonstick cooking spray. 4. In a medium bowl, beat the eggs, milk, salt, thyme, and black pepper well. 5. In the crock pot, layer half of the French bread. Top with half of the vegetable and ham mixture, and sprinkle with half of the Cheddar and Swiss cheeses. Repeat the layers. 6. Pour the egg mixture over everything, and sprinkle with the Parmesan cheese. 7. Cover and cook on low for 6 hours, or until the temperature registers 160°F (71°C) on a food thermometer and the mixture is set. 8. Using the foil sling, remove from the crock pot, and serve.

Streusel Cake

- 1 (16-ounce / 454-g) package pound cake mix, prepared according to package directions
- ¼ cup packed brown sugar
- 1 tablespoon flour
- ¼ cup chopped nuts
- 1 teaspoon cinnamon

1. Start by greasing and flouring a 2-pound (907-g) coffee can or a baking insert that fits into your crock pot. Make sure to coat it liberally to prevent sticking. Pour the prepared cake mix into the coffee can or baking insert. 2. In a separate small bowl, combine the brown sugar, flour, nuts, and cinnamon, mixing them well together. Sprinkle this mixture evenly over the top of the cake mix in the can or insert. 3. Carefully place the coffee tin or baking insert inside the crock pot. Cover the top of the tin or insert with several layers of paper towels to absorb moisture during cooking. 4. Place the lid on the crock pot and set it to cook on high for 3 to 4 hours, or until a toothpick inserted into the center of the cake comes out clean. 5. Once cooked, carefully remove the baking tin from the crock pot and allow it to cool for 30 minutes before cutting the cake into wedges for serving. Enjoy!

Overnight Apple Cinnamon Oatmeal

- 2 cups dry rolled oats
- 4 cups water
- 1 large apple, peeled and chopped
- 1 cup raisins
- 1 teaspoon cinnamon
- 1 to 2 tablespoons orange zest

1. Combine all ingredients in your crock pot. 2. Cover and cook on low 8 to 9 hours. 3. Serve topped with brown sugar, if you wish, and milk.

Cheesy Broccoli and Egg Casserole

Prep time: 15 minutes | Cook time: 2½ to 3 hours | Serves 6

- 1 (24-ounce / 680-g) carton small-curd cottage cheese
- 1 (10-ounce / 283-g) package frozen chopped broccoli, thawed and drained
- 2 cups shredded Cheddar cheese
- 6 eggs, beaten
- ⅓ cup flour
- ¼ cup butter, melted
- 3 tablespoons finely chopped onion
- ½ teaspoon salt
- Shredded cheese (optional)

1. Combine first 8 ingredients. Pour into greased crock pot. 2. Cover and cook on high 1 hour. Stir. Reduce heat to low. Cover and cook 2½ to 3 hours, or until temperature reaches 160ºF (71ºC) and eggs are set. 3. Sprinkle with cheese and serve.

Overnight Blueberry Cream Cheese French Toast

Prep time: 30 minutes | Cook time: 3 hours | Serves 12

- 8 eggs
- ½ cup plain yogurt
- ⅓ cup sour cream
- 1 teaspoon vanilla extract
- ½ teaspoon ground cinnamon
- 1 cup 2% milk

Blueberry Syrup:

- 1 cup sugar
- 2 tablespoons cornstarch
- 1 cup cold water

- ⅓ cup maple syrup
- 1 (1-pound / 454-g) loaf French bread, cubed
- 1½ cups fresh or frozen blueberries
- 12 ounces (340 g) cream cheese, cubed

- ¾ cup fresh or frozen blueberries, divided
- 1 tablespoon butter
- 1 tablespoon lemon juice

1. In a large bowl, whisk eggs, yogurt, sour cream, vanilla and cinnamon. Gradually whisk in milk and maple syrup until blended. 2. Place half of the bread in a greased 5- or 6-quart crock pot; layer with half of the blueberries, cream cheese and egg mixture. Repeat layers. Refrigerate, covered, overnight. 3. Remove from refrigerator 30 minutes before cooking. Cook, covered, on low 3 to 4 hours or until a knife inserted near the center comes out clean. 4. For syrup, in a small saucepan, mix sugar and cornstarch; stir in water until smooth. Stir in ¼ cup blueberries. Bring to a boil; cook and stir until berries pop, about 3 minutes. Remove from heat; stir in butter, lemon juice and remaining berries. Serve warm with French toast.

Coconut Protein Loaf

Prep time: 10 minutes | Cook time: 3 to 4 hours | Makes 8 slices

- 1 tablespoon butter, softened
- 6 large eggs
- ½ cup coconut oil, melted
- 1 teaspoon pure vanilla extract
- ¼ teaspoon liquid stevia
- 1 cup almond flour
- ½ cup coconut flour
- 1 ounce (28 g) protein powder
- 1 teaspoon baking powder

1. Grease an 8-by-4-inch loaf pan with the butter. 2. In a medium bowl, whisk together the eggs, oil, vanilla, and stevia until well blended. 3. In a small bowl, stir together the almond flour, coconut flour, protein powder, and baking powder until mixed. 4. Add the dry ingredients to the wet ingredients and stir to combine. 5. Spoon the batter into the loaf pan and place the loaf pan on a rack in the crock pot. 6. Cover and cook on low for 3 to 4 hours, until a knife inserted in the center comes out clean. 7. Cool the bread in the loaf pan for 15 minutes. Then remove the bread from the pan and place onto a wire rack to cool completely. 8. Store in a sealed container in the refrigerator for up to 1 week.

Toasted Maple Nut Granola

Prep time: 20 minutes | Cook time: 2 hours | Makes 5 to 6 cups

- ¾ cup extra-virgin olive oil, plus more for crock pot
- 4 cups old-fashioned rolled oats
- 1 cup raw shelled pistachios, almonds, walnuts, pecans, or hazelnuts, chopped if large
- ¼ cup packed brown sugar
- ½ teaspoon ground cinnamon
- ½ teaspoon coarse salt
- ½ cup pure maple syrup
- 1 tablespoon vanilla extract
- ½ cup dried apricots, dates, cherries, figs, raisins, blueberries, or cranberries, chopped if large

1. Brush the insert of a 5- to 6-quart crock pot with oil and preheat cooker. 2. Stir together oats, nuts, brown sugar, cinnamon, and ¼ teaspoon salt in the crock pot until well combined. Stir in oil, maple syrup, and vanilla, mixing until fully combined. Raise heat to high, partially cover, turning lid 45 degrees to allow moisture to escape, and cook on high, stirring every 30 minutes, until toasted and golden brown, about 2 hours (do not cook on low). After 1 hour, rotate cooker insert to prevent scorching. 3. Stir in dried fruit; then spread granola in a single layer on a rimmed baking sheet to cool completely. Sprinkle with remaining ¼ teaspoon salt, if desired. (Store in an airtight container at room temperature for up to 1 week.)

Breakfast Oatmeal

Prep time: 5 minutes | Cook time: 8 hours | Serves 6

- 2 cups dry rolled oats
- 4 cups water
- 1 teaspoon salt
- ½ to 1 cup chopped dates, or raisins, or cranberries, or a mixture of any of these fruits

1. In the crock pot, add all the ingredients, ensuring they are evenly distributed. 2. Cover the pot securely with the lid and set it to cook on low heat overnight, or for approximately 8 hours, allowing the flavors to meld beautifully as it cooks.

Slow-Cooked Maple Oatmeal Bake

Prep time: 10 minutes | Cook time: 2½ to 3 hours | Serves 4 to 6

- ⅓ cup oil
- ½ cup sugar
- 1 large egg, beaten
- 2 cups dry quick oats
- 1½ teaspoons baking powder
- ½ teaspoon salt
- ¾ cup milk

1. Pour the oil into the crock pot to grease bottom and sides. 2. Add remaining ingredients. Mix well. 3. Cook on low 2½ to 3 hours.

Peach French Toast Bake

Prep time: 15 minutes | Cook time: 6 hours | Serves 2

- Nonstick cooking spray
- ½ cup brown sugar
- 3 tablespoons butter
- 1 tablespoon water
- 1 teaspoon vanilla
- 8 slices French bread
- 1½ cups peeled sliced peaches
- 4 eggs
- 1 cup milk
- ¼ cup granulated sugar
- ½ teaspoon ground cinnamon
- ¼ teaspoon salt
- ⅔ cup chopped pecans

1. Start by lining the crock pot with heavy-duty foil and spray it generously with nonstick cooking spray to prevent sticking. 2. In a small saucepan over low heat, combine the brown sugar, butter, and water, bringing the mixture to a gentle simmer. Allow it to simmer for about 5 minutes, stirring constantly until it thickens into a syrup. Once done, remove it from the heat and stir in the vanilla extract. 3. In the prepared crock pot, create layers by alternating between pieces of bread and sliced peaches, drizzling each layer with some of the brown sugar syrup for added sweetness. 4. In a separate medium bowl, whisk together the eggs, milk, granulated sugar, cinnamon, and salt until well blended. Pour this egg mixture evenly over the layered bread and peaches in the crock pot, then sprinkle the top with chopped pecans for a crunchy texture. 5. Cover the crock pot and set it to cook on low for 6 hours, or until the mixture is firm and reaches an internal temperature of 160ºF (71ºC) on a food thermometer. 6. Once cooked, carefully remove the dessert from the crock pot, slice it into portions, and serve warm.

Slow-Cooked Cinnamon Rolls with Lemon Glaze

Prep time: 20 minutes | Cook time: 1½ hours | Serves 10 to 12

Buns:

- 6 tablespoons unsalted butter, room temperature, plus more for brushing
- 1⅓ cups warm water (about 110ºF / 43ºC)
- 1 tablespoon active dry yeast
- 2 tablespoons honey
- 3½ cups all-purpose flour, plus more for work surface
- 2 teaspoon coarse salt
- ¾ cup granulated sugar
- ¼ cup plus 2 tablespoons packed brown sugar
- 1 tablespoon ground cinnamon

Glaze:

- 3 cups confectioners' sugar
- Juice of ½ lemon
- 2 teaspoon vanilla extract
- ¼ cup plus 2 tablespoons milk

Make the Buns: 1. Brush the insert of a 5- to 6-quart crock pot with butter. Line bottom with parchment paper and brush paper with butter. 2. Combine the warm water, yeast, and honey in a bowl; let stand until foamy, about 5 minutes. Add flour and salt. With an electric mixer on low, mix until just combined. Increase speed to medium and mix for 5 minutes; let stand 10 minutes. Combine butter, both sugars, and cinnamon in a bowl; mix until smooth. 3. Preheat the crock pot. Turn dough out onto a lightly floured work surface and roll into a rectangle, about 9 by 15 inches. Sprinkle dough evenly with cinnamon-sugar mixture. Starting from one long side, roll into a log, pinching seams to seal in filling. Slice log into 10 to 12 rounds, each about 1½ inches thick. 4. Arrange rolls, cut side down, in the cooker. Wrap lid tightly with a clean kitchen towel, gathering ends at top (to absorb condensation). Cover and cook on high until cooked through, 1½ hours (we prefer to bake these on high). After 1 hour, rotate cooker insert to prevent scorching. Turn out onto a wire rack to cool before serving. Make the Glaze: 5. With an electric mixer, whisk confectioners' sugar, lemon juice, and vanilla until smooth. Slowly add ¼ cup milk and beat on medium. Add more milk, a drop at a time up to 2 tablespoons, to reach desired consistency. Drizzle rolls with glaze just before serving.

Crock Pot Egg–Potato Bake

Prep time: 20 minutes | Cook time: 6 hours | Serves 2

- 2 slices bacon, chopped
- 1 cup pork sausage
- 1 onion, chopped
- 1 cup sliced button mushrooms
- 2 garlic cloves, minced
- 1 orange bell pepper, chopped
- Nonstick cooking spray
- 3 russet potatoes, peeled and sliced
- 1 cup shredded Havarti cheese
- ½ cup shredded Colby cheese
- 5 eggs, beaten
- 1 cup milk
- ½ teaspoon salt
- ½ teaspoon dried thyme leaves
- ⅛ teaspoon freshly ground black pepper

1. In a medium skillet over medium heat, cook the bacon and sausage until the bacon is crisp and the sausage is browned, 10 minutes or so, stirring frequently. Remove the bacon and sausage to a paper towel–lined plate to drain. Remove and discard all but 1 tablespoon of drippings from the pan. 2. In the same skillet over medium heat, cook the onion, mushrooms, and garlic in the remaining drippings until tender, about 5 minutes. Remove from the heat and add the bell pepper, bacon, and sausage. 3. Line the crock pot with heavy-duty foil and spray with the nonstick cooking spray. 4. In the crock pot, layer the potatoes, bacon mixture, and cheeses. 5. In a medium bowl, beat the eggs, milk, salt, thyme, and pepper. Pour the egg mixture into the crock pot. 6. Cover and cook on low for 6 hours, or until the temperature reaches 160ºF (71ºC) on a food thermometer. 7. Using the foil, remove from the crock pot, cut into squares, and serve.

Carrot Cake Oatmeal

Prep time: 10 minutes | Cook time: 6 hours | Serves 8

- 4½ cups water
- 1 (20-ounce / 567-g) can crushed pineapple, undrained
- 2 cups shredded carrots
- 1 cup steel-cut oats
- 1 cup raisins
- 2 teaspoons ground cinnamon
- 1 teaspoon pumpkin pie spice
- Brown sugar (optional)

1. Begin by spraying the interior of a 4-quart crock pot with cooking spray to prevent sticking. 2. In the pot, combine the first seven ingredients, ensuring they are mixed well. 3. Cover the crock pot and set it to cook on low for 6 to 8 hours, or until the oats are tender and the liquid has been absorbed. 4. If desired, sprinkle with brown sugar before serving for added sweetness.

Nutty Oatmeal

Prep time: 10 minutes | Cook time: 7 hours | Makes 7 cups

- 1 cup chopped walnuts
- Nonstick cooking spray
- 2 cups rolled oats (not instant or quick cooking)
- 1 cup raisins
- 3 cups almond milk
- 1½ cups apple juice
- ⅓ cup honey
- ⅓ cup brown sugar
- ½ teaspoon ground cinnamon
- ¼ teaspoon ground nutmeg
- ¼ teaspoon salt

1. Begin by toasting the walnuts in a small saucepan over medium-low heat, stirring frequently for about 2 minutes until they become fragrant. 2. Next, spray the inside of the crock pot with nonstick cooking spray to prevent sticking. 3. In the crock pot, combine the toasted walnuts, oats, and raisins, mixing them together evenly. 4. In a large mixing bowl, whisk together the almond milk, apple juice, honey, brown sugar, cinnamon, nutmeg, and salt until well blended. Pour this mixture over the ingredients in the crock pot. 5. Cover the crock pot and cook on low for 7 hours, or until the oatmeal has thickened and the oats are tender. Serve warm and enjoy!

Vegetable Omelet

Prep time: 15 minutes | Cook time: 4 to 5 hours | Serves 8

- 1 tablespoon extra-virgin olive oil
- 10 eggs
- ½ cup heavy (whipping) cream
- 1 teaspoon minced garlic
- ¼ teaspoon salt
- ⅛ teaspoon freshly ground black pepper
- ½ cup chopped cauliflower
- ½ cup chopped broccoli
- 1 red bell pepper, chopped
- 1 scallion, white and green parts, chopped
- 4 ounces (113 g) goat cheese, crumbled
- 2 tablespoons chopped parsley, for garnish

1. Begin by lightly greasing the insert of the crock pot with olive oil to prevent sticking. 2. In a medium bowl, whisk together the eggs, heavy cream, garlic, salt, and pepper until well combined. Stir in the cauliflower, broccoli, red bell pepper, and scallion, ensuring all vegetables are evenly coated. Pour this mixture into the prepared crock pot and sprinkle goat cheese over the top. 3. Cover the crock pot and set it to cook on low for 4 to 5 hours, allowing the flavors to meld and the vegetables to cook through. 4. Once done, serve the dish warm, garnished with freshly chopped parsley for added flavor and color.

Banana Bread Casserole

Prep time: 15 minutes | Cook time: 6 hours | Serves 2

- Nonstick cooking spray
- 6 slices banana bread, cubed
- 6 slices French bread, cubed
- 1 banana, sliced
- 4 slices bacon, cooked and crumbled
- ½ cup chopped pecans
- 4 eggs, beaten
- 1½ cups milk
- ⅓ cup sugar
- 2 tablespoons honey
- 1 teaspoon ground cinnamon
- 1 teaspoon vanilla
- ¼ teaspoon salt

1. Start by applying a light coat of nonstick cooking spray to the interior of the crock pot to prevent sticking. 2. Next, layer the ingredients in the crock pot, starting with slices of banana bread, followed by French bread, banana slices, crispy bacon, and finally, chopped pecans. 3. In a separate medium bowl, whisk together the eggs, milk, sugar, honey, cinnamon, vanilla extract, and salt until well combined. Pour this egg mixture evenly over the layered ingredients in the crock pot. 4. Cover the crock pot with its lid and set it to cook on low for about 6 hours, or until a food thermometer indicates that the internal temperature has reached 160ºF (71ºC). Once done, serve warm and enjoy!

Granola

Prep time: 15 minutes | Cook time: 4 hours | Makes 8 cups

- Nonstick cooking spray
- 4 cups old-fashioned rolled oats
- 1 cup slivered almonds
- 1 cup coarsely chopped pecans
- 1 cup sunflower seeds
- 1 cup shredded coconut
- ⅓ cup butter or coconut oil
- 2 tablespoons safflower oil
- ½ cup honey
- ⅓ cup brown sugar
- 2 teaspoons vanilla
- 1 teaspoon ground cinnamon
- ½ teaspoon salt

1. Start by spraying the inside of the crock pot with nonstick cooking spray. 2. In the crock pot, mix together the oats, almonds, pecans, sunflower seeds, and coconut until well combined. 3. In a medium saucepan set over low heat, melt the butter along with the safflower oil, honey, brown sugar, vanilla extract, cinnamon, and salt. Stir gently for about 5 minutes until the butter is fully melted. 4. Pour the melted butter mixture over the dry ingredients in the crock pot and stir thoroughly to ensure everything is evenly coated. 5. Cover the crock pot, leaving the lid slightly ajar to allow steam to escape, and cook on low for 3 to 4 hours, stirring every hour if possible, until the mixture turns a golden brown color. 6. Once cooked, transfer the granola to greased baking sheets, spreading it into an even layer. Allow it to cool before breaking it into pieces. Serve immediately or store in an airtight container at room temperature for later enjoyment.

Welsh Rarebit

Prep time: 10 minutes | Cook time: 1½ to 2½ hours | Serves 6 to 8

- 1 (12-ounce / 340-g) can beer
- 1 tablespoon dry mustard
- 1 teaspoon Worcestershire sauce
- ½ teaspoon salt
- ⅛ teaspoon black or white pepper
- 1 pound (454 g) American
- cheese, cubed
- 1 pound (454 g) sharp Cheddar cheese, cubed
- English muffins or toast
- Tomato slices
- Bacon, cooked until crisp
- Fresh steamed asparagus spears

1. In the crock pot, mix together the beer, mustard, Worcestershire sauce, salt, and pepper until well combined. Cover the pot and set it to cook on high for 1 to 2 hours, or until the mixture reaches a boil. 2. Gradually add the cheese to the bubbling mixture, incorporating it a little at a time while stirring constantly until all the cheese has completely melted. 3. Leave the lid off and continue to heat the mixture on high for an additional 20 to 30 minutes, stirring frequently to ensure a smooth consistency. 4. Serve the cheese sauce hot over toasted English muffins or triangular pieces of toasted bread. For an attractive presentation, garnish the dish with slices of fresh tomatoes, crispy bacon strips, and tender steamed asparagus spears.

Slow-Cooked Mixed Fruit Compote

Prep time: 5 minutes | Cook time: 2 to 7 hours | Serves 8 to 9

- 1 (12-ounce / 340-g) package dried apricots
- 1 (12-ounce / 340-g) package pitted dried plums
- 1 (11-ounce / 312-g) can mandarin oranges in light
- syrup, undrained
- 1 (29-ounce / 822-g) can sliced peaches in light syrup, undrained
- ¼ cup white raisins
- 10 maraschino cherries

1. Combine all ingredients in crock pot. Mix well. 2. Cover. Cook on low 6 to 7 hours, or on high 2 to 3 hours.

Blueberry Apple Waffle Topping

Prep time: 10 minutes | Cook time: 3 hours | Serves 10 to 12

- 1 quart natural applesauce, unsweetened
- 2 Granny Smith apples, unpeeled, cored, and sliced
- 1 pint fresh or frozen blueberries
- ½ tablespoon ground cinnamon
- ½ cup pure maple syrup
- 1 teaspoon almond flavoring
- ½ cup walnuts, chopped
- Nonfat cooking spray

1. In a crock pot sprayed with nonfat cooking spray, combine the applesauce, diced apples, and blueberries, stirring until well mixed. 2. Sprinkle in the cinnamon and drizzle the maple syrup over the fruit mixture, then stir to incorporate. 3. Cover the crock pot and cook on low for 3 hours to allow the flavors to meld. 4. Just before serving, stir in the almond flavoring and chopped walnuts for added texture and flavor.

Overnight Hominy Breakfast Porridge

Prep time: 5 minutes | Cook time: 8 hours | Serves 5

- 1 cup dry cracked hominy
- 1 teaspoon salt
- Black pepper (optional)
- 3 cups water
- 2 tablespoons butter

1. Stir all ingredients together in a greased crock pot. 2. Cover and cook on low 8 hours, or overnight. 3. Serve warm for breakfast.

Creamy Crock Pot Polenta Slices

Prep time: 10 minutes | Cook time:2 to 9 hours | Serves 8 to 10

- 4 tablespoons melted butter, divided
- ¼ teaspoon paprika
- 6 cups boiling water
- 2 cups dry cornmeal
- 2 teaspoons salt

1. Use 1 tablespoon butter to lightly grease the inside of the crock pot. Sprinkle in paprika. Turn to high setting. 2. Add remaining ingredients to crock pot in the order listed, including 1 tablespoon butter. Stir well. 3. Cover and cook on high 2 to 3 hours, or on low 6 to 9 hours. Stir occasionally. 4. Pour hot cooked polenta into 2 lightly greased loaf pans. Chill 8 hours or overnight. 5. To serve, cut into ¼-inch-thick slices. Melt 2 tablespoons butter in large nonstick skillet, then lay in slices and cook until browned. Turn to brown other side. 6. For breakfast, serve with your choice of sweetener.

Crustless Wild Mushroom–Kale Quiche

Prep time: 10 minutes | Cook time: 5 to 6 hours | Serves 8

- 1 tablespoon extra-virgin olive oil
- 12 eggs
- 1 cup heavy (whipping) cream
- 1 tablespoon chopped fresh thyme
- 1 tablespoon chopped fresh chives
- ¼ teaspoon freshly ground black pepper
- ⅛ teaspoon salt
- 2 cups coarsely chopped wild mushrooms (shiitake, portobello, oyster, enoki)
- 1 cup chopped kale
- 1 cup shredded Swiss cheese

1. Begin by lightly greasing the insert of the crock pot with olive oil to prevent sticking. 2. In a medium bowl, whisk together the eggs, heavy cream, thyme, chives, pepper, and salt until well combined. Stir in the mushrooms and kale until evenly distributed. 3. Pour the egg and vegetable mixture into the prepared crock pot and sprinkle the cheese on top. 4. Cover the crock pot and cook on low for 5 to 6 hours, allowing the flavors to meld and the dish to set. 5. Once cooked, serve warm and enjoy!

Breakfast Prunes

Prep time: 10 minutes | Cook time: 8 to 10 hours | Serves 6

- 2 cups orange juice
- ¼ cup orange marmalade
- 1 teaspoon ground cinnamon
- ¼ teaspoon ground cloves
- ¼ teaspoon ground nutmeg
- 1 cup water
- 1 (12-ounce / 340-g) package pitted dried prunes
- 2 thin lemon slices

1. In a crock pot, combine the orange juice, marmalade, cinnamon, cloves, nutmeg, and water, stirring well to mix all the ingredients. 2. Add the prunes and lemon slices, incorporating them into the mixture. 3. Cover the crock pot and cook on low for 8 to 10 hours, or you can prepare it overnight. 4. Serve the dish warm as a breakfast option or enjoy it warm or chilled as a delightful side dish with a meal later in the day.

Slow-Cooked Spiced Pumpkin Pudding

Prep time: 15 minutes | Cook time: 6 to 7 hours | Serves 8

- ¼ cup melted butter, divided
- 2½ cups canned pumpkin purée
- 2 cups coconut milk
- 4 eggs
- 1 tablespoon pure vanilla extract
- 1 cup almond flour
- ½ cup granulated erythritol
- 2 ounces (57 g) protein powder
- 1 teaspoon baking powder
- 1 teaspoon ground cinnamon
- ¼ teaspoon ground nutmeg
- Pinch ground cloves

1. Lightly grease the insert of the crock pot with 1 tablespoon of the butter. 2. In a large bowl, whisk together the remaining butter, pumpkin, coconut milk, eggs, and vanilla until well blended. 3. In a small bowl, stir together the almond flour, erythritol, protein powder, baking powder, cinnamon, nutmeg, and cloves. 4. Add the dry ingredients to the wet ingredients and stir to combine. 5. Pour the mixture into the insert. 6. Cover and cook on low for 6 to 7 hours. 7. Serve warm.

Crock Pot Frittata Provencal

Prep time: 30 minutes | Cook time: 3 hours | Serves 6

- ½ cup water
- 1 tablespoon olive oil
- 1 medium Yukon Gold potato, peeled and sliced
- 1 small onion, thinly sliced
- ½ teaspoon smoked paprika
- 12 eggs
- 1 teaspoon minced fresh thyme or ¼ teaspoon dried
- thyme
- 1 teaspoon hot pepper sauce
- ½ teaspoon salt
- ¼ teaspoon pepper
- 1 (4-ounce / 113-g) log fresh goat cheese, coarsely crumbled, divided
- ½ cup chopped soft sun-dried tomatoes (not packed in oil)

1. Begin by layering two 24-inch pieces of aluminum foil; fold up the foil starting from a long side to create a 1-inch wide strip and then shape this strip into a coil to form a rack for the bottom of a 6-quart oval crock pot. Add water to the crock pot and set the foil rack in the water. 2. In a large skillet, heat the oil over medium-high heat. Add the potato and onion, cooking and stirring for 5 to 7 minutes or until the potato is lightly browned. Stir in the paprika, then transfer the mixture to a greased 1½-quart baking dish (ensure the dish fits in the crock pot). 3. In a large bowl, whisk together the eggs, thyme, pepper sauce, salt, and pepper; then stir in 2 ounces (57 g) of cheese. Pour this egg mixture over the potato mixture and top with the tomatoes and the remaining goat cheese. Place the baking

dish on the foil rack. 4. Cover the crock pot and cook on low for 3 hours or until the eggs are set and a knife inserted near the center comes out clean.

Pumpkin-Pecan N' Oatmeal

Prep time: 10 minutes | Cook time: 8 hours | Serves 4

- 1 tablespoon coconut oil
- 3 cups cubed pumpkin, cut into 1-inch chunks
- 2 cups coconut milk
- ½ cup ground pecans
- 1 ounce (28 g) plain protein powder
- 2 tablespoons granulated erythritol
- 1 teaspoon maple extract
- ½ teaspoon ground nutmeg
- ¼ teaspoon ground cinnamon
- Pinch ground allspice

1. Begin by lightly greasing the insert of a slow cooker with coconut oil to prevent sticking. 2. Next, add the pumpkin, coconut milk, pecans, protein powder, erythritol, maple extract, nutmeg, cinnamon, and allspice into the insert, ensuring all ingredients are well combined. 3. Cover the slow cooker and set it to cook on low for 8 hours, allowing the flavors to meld together beautifully. 4. After cooking, stir the mixture or use a potato masher to achieve your desired texture, then serve warm and enjoy!

Slow-Cooked Ranchero Egg Bake

Prep time: 10 minutes | Cook time: 3 hours | Serves 8

- 1 tablespoon extra-virgin olive oil
- 10 eggs
- 1 cup heavy (whipping) cream
- 1 cup shredded Monterey Jack cheese, divided
- 1 cup prepared or homemade salsa
- 1 scallion, green and white parts, chopped
- 1 jalapeño pepper, chopped
- ½ teaspoon chili powder
- ½ teaspoon salt
- 1 avocado, chopped, for garnish
- 1 tablespoon chopped cilantro, for garnish

1. Lightly grease the insert of the crock pot with the olive oil. 2. In a large bowl, whisk together the eggs, heavy cream, ½ cup of the cheese, salsa, scallion, jalapeño, chili powder, and salt. Pour the mixture into the insert and sprinkle the top with the remaining ½ cup of cheese. 3. Cover and cook until the eggs are firm, about 3 hours on low. 4. Let the eggs cool slightly, then cut into wedges and serve garnished with avocado and cilantro.

Slow-Cooked Fruited Oatmeal with Nuts

Prep time: 15 minutes | Cook time: 6 hours | Serves 6

- 3 cups water
- 2 cups old-fashioned oats
- 2 cups chopped apples
- 1 cup dried cranberries
- 1 cup fat-free milk
- 2 teaspoons butter, melted
- 1 teaspoon pumpkin pie spice
- 1 teaspoon ground cinnamon
- 6 tablespoons chopped almonds, toasted
- 6 tablespoons chopped pecans, toasted
- Additional fat-free milk

1. In a 3-quart crock pot that has been coated with cooking spray, combine the first eight ingredients thoroughly. Cover the pot and set it to cook on low for 6 to 8 hours, or until the liquid has been absorbed and the oatmeal is cooked through. 2. Once cooked, spoon the oatmeal into bowls. For serving, sprinkle with almonds and pecans, and drizzle with additional milk if desired. Enjoy your delicious and nutritious meal!

Southwest Breakfast Casserole

Prep time: 10 minutes | Cook time: 8 hours | Serves 2

- 1 teaspoon butter, at room temperature, or extra-virgin olive oil
- 2 eggs
- 2 egg whites
- 1 teaspoon ground cumin
- 1 teaspoon smoked paprika
- ⅛ teaspoon sea salt
- Freshly ground black pepper
- ½ cup shredded pepper Jack cheese
- ½ cup canned fire-roasted diced tomatoes
- ½ cup canned black beans, drained and rinsed
- 1 teaspoon minced garlic
- 3 corn tortillas
- ¼ cup fresh cilantro, for garnish

1. Begin by greasing the inside of the crock pot with butter to prevent sticking. 2. In a small bowl, whisk together the eggs, egg whites, cumin, paprika, salt, and a few grinds of black pepper until well combined. 3. In another small bowl, mix together the cheese, diced tomatoes, black beans, and minced garlic for the filling. 4. Start assembling by placing one corn tortilla in the bottom of the crock pot, then layer half of the cheese and bean mixture on top. Pour one-third of the egg mixture over this layer. Next, add another tortilla on top. 5. Repeat the process by layering the remaining cheese and bean mixture over the second tortilla, followed by another one-third of the egg mixture. Place the final tortilla on top, and pour the remaining egg mixture over it. 6. Cover the crock pot

and cook on low for 8 hours or overnight. Before serving, garnish with fresh cilantro for added flavor.

Crockpot Asparagus and Bacon Frittata

Prep time: 10 minutes | Cook time: 4 to 5 hours | Serves 8

- 1 tablespoon extra-virgin olive oil
- 10 eggs
- ¾ cup coconut milk
- ½ teaspoon salt
- ¼ teaspoon freshly ground
- black pepper
- 2 teaspoons chopped fresh dill
- 2 cups chopped asparagus spears
- 1 cup chopped cooked bacon

1. Lightly grease the insert of the crock pot with the olive oil. 2. In a medium bowl, whisk together the eggs, coconut milk, salt, pepper, and dill. Stir in the asparagus and bacon. Pour the mixture into the crock pot. 3. Cover and cook on low for 4 to 5 hours. 4. Serve warm.

Chocolate-Cherry-Stuffed French Toast

Prep time: 15 minutes | Cook time: 6 hours | Serves 2

- Nonstick cooking spray
- 8 slices French bread
- ¾ cup mascarpone cheese
- ½ cup cherry preserves
- ¾ cup semisweet chocolate chips, melted
- 1 cup sliced pitted fresh
- cherries
- 5 eggs, beaten
- 1 cup milk
- 1 teaspoon vanilla
- ½ teaspoon ground cinnamon
- ¼ teaspoon salt

1. Start by lining the crock pot with heavy-duty foil and spraying it with nonstick cooking spray to ensure easy removal later. 2. Take each slice of bread and spread mascarpone cheese on one side, followed by cherry preserves, and drizzle melted chocolate over the top. 3. Cut the prepared bread slices in half and layer them in the crock pot, adding fresh cherries in between the layers. 4. In a medium bowl, whisk together the eggs, milk, vanilla extract, cinnamon, and salt until well combined, then pour the egg mixture over the bread and cherries in the crock pot. 5. Cover the crock pot and set it to cook on low for 6 hours, or until the mixture is set and reaches an internal temperature of 160°F (71°C). Once done, carefully remove the dish from the crock pot using the foil, slice, and serve.

Crock Pot Zucchini-Carrot Bread

Prep time: 15 minutes | Cook time: 3 to 5 hours | Makes 8 slices

- 2 teaspoons butter, for greasing pan
- 1 cup almond flour
- 1 cup granulated erythritol
- ½ cup coconut flour
- 1½ teaspoons baking powder
- 1 teaspoon ground cinnamon
- ½ teaspoon ground nutmeg
- ½ teaspoon baking soda
- ¼ teaspoon salt
- 4 eggs
- ½ cup butter, melted
- 1 tablespoon pure vanilla extract
- 1½ cups finely grated zucchini
- ½ cup finely grated carrot

1. Lightly grease a 9-by-5-inch loaf pan with the butter and set aside. 2. Place a small rack in the bottom of your crock pot. 3. In a large bowl, stir together the almond flour, erythritol, coconut flour, baking powder, cinnamon, nutmeg, baking soda, and salt until well mixed. 4. In a separate medium bowl, whisk together the eggs, melted butter, and vanilla until well blended. 5. Add the wet ingredients to dry ingredients and stir to combine. 6. Stir in the zucchini and carrot. 7. Spoon the batter into the prepared loaf pan. 8. Place the loaf pan on the rack in the bottom of the crock pot, cover, and cook on high for 3 hours. 9. Remove the loaf pan, let the bread cool completely, and serve.

Slow-Cooker Enchiladas Verde

Prep time: 20 minutes | Cook time: 4 to 5 hours | Serves 6 to 8

- 2 tablespoons vegetable oil
- 1 medium onion, finely chopped
- 1 Anaheim chile pepper, seeded and finely chopped
- 4 tablespoons finely chopped fresh cilantro
- 3 cups tomatillo salsa
- ½ cup chicken broth
- 2½ cups finely shredded mild Cheddar cheese
- 2 cups finely shredded Monterey Jack or Pepper Jack cheese
- 2 cups crumbled queso fresco
- 2 cups sour cream
- 12 (6-inch) round white or yellow corn tortillas, cut in strips or roughly torn

1. Coat the insert of a 5- to 7-quart crock pot with nonstick cooking spray or line it with a slow-cooker liner according to the manufacturer's directions. 2. Heat the oil in a medium saucepan over medium-high heat. Add the onion and chile and sauté until they are softened and fragrant, 3 to 5 minutes. 3. Add 2 tablespoons of the cilantro, the salsa, and broth and simmer for 30 minutes, until the sauce is reduced and thickened a bit. Remove from the heat and set aside to cool slightly. Put the Cheddar and Monterey Jack cheese in a mixing bowl and stir to combine. 4. Put the queso fresco, the remaining 2 tablespoons cilantro, and the sour cream in another bowl and stir to combine. Spoon a thin layer of the sauce on the bottom of the crock pot insert. Layer one-third of the tortillas evenly on the bottom of the crock pot. 5. Spread half the queso fresco mixture over the tortillas and top with one-third of the shredded cheese. Repeat, layering the tortillas, sauce, queso fresco, and shredded cheese. Finish layering the remaining tortillas, sauce, and shredded cheese. Cover and cook on low for 3 to 4 hours, until the casserole is cooked through and the cheese is bubbling. Remove the cover and cook for an additional 30 to 45 minutes. 6. Serve from the cooker set on warm.

Spiced Pumpkin Protein Bars

Prep time: 15 minutes | Cook time: 3 hours | Makes 8 bars

Crust:
- 5 tablespoons butter, softened, divided
- ¾ cup unsweetened shredded coconut
- ½ cup almond flour
- ¼ cup granulated erythritol

Filling:
- 1 (28-ounce / 794-g) can pumpkin purée
- 1 cup heavy (whipping) cream
- 4 eggs
- 1 ounce (28 g) protein powder
- 1 teaspoon pure vanilla extract
- 4 drops liquid stevia
- 1 teaspoon ground cinnamon
- ½ teaspoon ground ginger
- ¼ teaspoon ground nutmeg
- Pinch ground cloves
- Pinch salt

Make the Crust: 1. Lightly grease the bottom of the insert of the crock pot with 1 tablespoon of the butter. 2. In a small bowl, stir together the coconut, almond flour, erythritol, and remaining butter until the mixture forms into coarse crumbs. 3. Press the crumbs into the bottom of the insert evenly to form a crust. Make the Filling: 4. In a medium bowl, stir together the pumpkin, heavy cream, eggs, protein powder, vanilla, stevia, cinnamon, ginger, nutmeg, cloves, and salt until well blended. 5. Spread the filling evenly over the crust. 6. Cover and cook on low for 3 hours. 7. Uncover and let cool for 30 minutes. Then place the insert in the refrigerator until completely chilled, about 2 hours. 8. Cut into squares and store them in the refrigerator in a sealed container for up to 5 days.

Chapter **2**

Beans and Grains

Chapter 2 Beans and Grains

Smoky Baked Bean Casserole

Prep time: 20 minutes | Cook time: 3 to 6 hours | Serves 10

- 1 pound (454 g) ground beef
- ¼ cup minced onions
- 1 cup ketchup
- 4 (15-ounce / 425-g) cans pork and beans
- 1 cup brown sugar
- 2 tablespoons liquid smoke
- 1 tablespoon Worcestershire sauce

1. Brown beef and onions in skillet. Drain. Spoon meat and onions into crock pot. 2. Add remaining ingredients and stir well. 3. Cover. Cook on high 3 hours, or on low 5 to 6 hours.

Risotto alla Milanese

Prep time: 10 minutes | Cook time: 2½ hours | Serves 4 to 6

- ½ cup (1 stick) unsalted butter
- 2 tablespoons olive oil
- 1 teaspoon saffron threads
- ½ cup finely chopped shallots (about 4 medium)
- 1½ cups Arborio or
- Carnaroli rice
- ¼ cup dry white wine or vermouth
- 4 cups chicken broth
- ½ cup freshly grated Parmigiano-Reggiano cheese

1. Start by coating the insert of a 5- to 7-quart crock pot with nonstick cooking spray, or alternatively, line it with a slow-cooker liner according to the manufacturer's instructions. 2. In a large saucepan over medium-high heat, melt ¼ cup of butter along with the oil. Once melted, add the saffron and shallots, cooking while stirring until the shallots become soft. Next, add the rice, cooking it until it's coated in the buttery mixture and begins to look opaque. Pour in the wine and let it evaporate completely. 3. Afterward, transfer the contents of the saucepan into the slow-cooker insert. Add the broth and stir to mix everything well. Cover the crock pot and cook on high for 2½ hours. At the 2-hour mark, check the risotto to ensure that the broth hasn't evaporated. By the end of the cooking time, the risotto should be tender and creamy. Stir in the remaining ¼ cup of butter and ¼ cup of cheese until combined. 4. Serve the risotto hot, with the remaining cheese offered on the side for added flavor.

Scandinavian-Style Sweet and Savory Beans

Prep time: 50 minutes | Cook time: 8 hours | Serves 8

- 1 pound (454 g) dried pinto beans
- 6 cups water
- 12 ounces (340 g) bacon, or 1 ham hock
- 1 onion, chopped
- 2 to 3 garlic cloves, minced
- ¼ teaspoon pepper
- 1 teaspoon salt
- ¼ cup molasses
- 1 cup ketchup
- Tabasco to taste
- 1 teaspoon Worcestershire sauce
- ¾ cup brown sugar
- ½ cup cider vinegar
- ¼ teaspoon dry mustard

1. Soak beans in water in soup pot for 8 hours. Bring beans to boil and cook 1½ to 2 hours, or until soft. Drain, reserving liquid. 2. Combine all ingredients in crock pot, using just enough bean liquid to cover everything. Cook on low 5 to 6 hours. If using ham hock, debone, cut ham into bite-sized pieces, and mix into beans.

Earthy Whole Brown Lentil Dhal

Prep time: 10 minutes | Cook time: 6 to 8 hours | Serves 6

- 6⅓ cups hot water
- 2 cups whole brown lentils
- 1 tablespoon ghee
- 1 teaspoon freshly grated ginger
- 1 teaspoon sea salt
- 1 teaspoon turmeric
- 7 to 8 ounces (198 to 227 g)
- canned tomatoes
- 4 garlic cloves, finely chopped
- 1 or 2 fresh green chiles, finely chopped
- 1 onion, chopped
- 1 teaspoon garam masala
- Handful fresh coriander leaves, chopped

1. Rinse and clean the lentils thoroughly, then allow them to drain. 2. Set the crock pot to high heat and add all ingredients except the garam masala and fresh coriander leaves. 3. Cover the crock pot and cook on high for 6 hours or on low for 8 hours. 4. Before serving, stir in the garam masala and fresh coriander leaves, then enjoy your dish.

Sweet and Tangy Mixed Bean Medley

Prep time: 10 minutes | Cook time: 4 to 5 hours | Serves 6

- 1 (16-ounce / 454-g) can kidney beans, drained
- 1 (15½-ounce / 439-g) can baked beans, undrained
- 1 pint home-frozen, or 1 (1-pound / 454-g) package frozen, lima beans
- 1 pint home-frozen, or 1 (1-pound / 454-g) package frozen, green beans
- 4 slices lean turkey bacon, browned and crumbled
- ½ cup ketchup
- ⅓ cup sugar
- ⅓ cup brown sugar
- 2 tablespoons vinegar
- ½ teaspoon salt

1. Combine beans and bacon in crock pot. 2. Stir together remaining ingredients. Add to beans and mix well. 3. Cover. Cook on low 4 to 5 hours.

White Beans with Kale

Prep time: 15 minutes | Cook time: 7½ hours | Serves 2

- 1 onion, chopped
- 1 leek, white part only, sliced
- 2 celery stalks, sliced
- 2 garlic cloves, minced
- 1 cup dried white lima beans or cannellini beans, sorted and rinsed
- 2 cups vegetable broth
- ½ teaspoon salt
- ½ teaspoon dried thyme leaves
- ⅛ teaspoon freshly ground black pepper
- 3 cups torn kale

1. In the crock pot, combine all ingredients except the kale. 2. Cover and cook on low for 7 hours, or until the beans are tender. 3. Once the beans are tender, add the kale and stir to combine. 4. Cover and cook on high for an additional 30 minutes, or until the kale is tender but still firm, then serve.

Quick and Simple Baked Beans

Prep time: 10 minutes | Cook time: 2 hours | Serves 8

- 2 (16-ounce / 454-g) cans baked beans
- ¼ cup brown sugar
- ½ teaspoon dried mustard
- ½ cup ketchup
- 2 small onions, chopped
- 1 teaspoon Worcestershire sauce

1. Combine all ingredients in crock pot. 2. Cover. Cook on high 2 hours.

Crock Pot Kidney Beans

Prep time: 15 minutes | Cook time: 6 to 7 hours | Serves 12

- 2 (30-ounce / 850-g) cans kidney beans, rinsed and drained
- 1 (28-ounce / 794-g) can diced tomatoes, drained
- 2 medium red bell peppers, chopped
- 1 cup ketchup
- ½ cup brown sugar
- ¼ cup honey
- ¼ cup molasses
- 1 tablespoon Worcestershire sauce
- 1 teaspoon dry mustard
- 2 medium red apples, cored, cut into pieces

1. In the crock pot, combine all ingredients except for the apples. 2. Cover the pot and set it to cook on low for 4 to 5 hours. 3. After the initial cooking time, stir in the apples. 4. Cover again and cook for an additional 2 hours.

Cornbread-Topped Chili Beans

Prep time: 20 minutes | Cook time: 3 hours | Serves 8

- 1 medium onion, chopped
- 1 medium green pepper, chopped
- 1 tablespoon canola oil
- 2 garlic cloves, minced
- 1 (16-ounce / 454-g) can kidney beans, rinsed and drained
- 1 (15-ounce / 425-g) can pinto beans, rinsed and drained
- 1 (14½-ounce / 411-g can) diced tomatoes, undrained
- 1 (8-ounce / 227-g can) tomato sauce
- 1 teaspoon chili powder
- ½ teaspoon pepper
- ⅛ teaspoon hot pepper sauce

Corn Bread Topping:

- 1 cup all-purpose flour
- 1 cup yellow cornmeal
- 1 tablespoon sugar
- 1½ teaspoons baking powder
- ½ teaspoon salt
- 2 eggs, lightly beaten
- 1¼ cups fat-free milk
- 1 (8¼-ounce / 234-g) can cream-style corn
- 3 tablespoons canola oil

1. In a large skillet, saute onion and green pepper in oil until tender. Add garlic; cook 1 minute longer. Transfer to a greased 5-quart crock pot. 2. Stir in the beans, tomatoes, tomato sauce, chili powder, pepper and pepper sauce. Cover and cook on high for 1 hour. 3. In a large bowl, combine the flour, cornmeal, sugar, baking powder and salt. Combine the eggs, milk, corn and oil; add to dry ingredients and mix well. Spoon evenly over bean mixture. 4. Cover and cook on high for 2 hours or until a toothpick inserted near the center of corn bread comes out clean.

Barbecued Lima Beans

- 1¼ cups dried lima beans
- Half a medium onion, chopped in large pieces
- ½ teaspoon salt
- ½ teaspoon dry mustard
- 1 teaspoon cider vinegar
- 2 tablespoons molasses
- ¼ cup chili sauce or medium salsa
- Several drops Tabasco sauce

1. Place the beans in a bowl and cover them with water. Allow the beans to soak overnight. Drain the beans, reserving 1 cup of the liquid. 2. Combine all ingredients in the crock pot, including the reserved 1 cup of bean liquid. 3. Cook on low for 8 to 10 hours until the beans are tender.

Savory Farro and Mushroom Pilaf

- 1 cup farro, rinsed
- 1 onion, chopped
- 1 cup sliced shiitake mushrooms
- 1 leek, white part only, chopped
- 3 garlic cloves, minced
- 2½ cups vegetable broth
- 1 teaspoon dried marjoram leaves
- ½ teaspoon salt
- ⅛ teaspoon freshly ground black pepper
- 2 tablespoons butter

1. In the crock pot, combine all the ingredients except the butter, and stir. 2. Cover and cook on low for 6 hours, or until the farro is tender. 3. Stir in the butter and serve.

Apple-Cranberry Multigrain Hot Cereal

- 2 medium apples, peeled and chopped
- 1 cup sugar
- 1 cup fresh cranberries
- ½ cup wheat berries
- ½ cup quinoa, rinsed
- ½ cup oat bran
- ½ cup medium pearl barley
- ½ cup chopped walnuts
- ½ cup packed brown sugar
- 1½ to 2 teaspoons ground cinnamon
- 6 cups water
- Milk

1. Place the first 11 ingredients into a 3-quart slow cooker. Stir to mix everything well. 2. Cover the slow cooker and set it to cook on low heat for 4 to 5 hours, or until the grains have softened and fully cooked through. 3. Once done, dish it up and enjoy with a splash of milk on top.

Slow-Cooked Herb-Infused Rice

- 3 chicken bouillon cubes
- 3 cups water
- 1½ cups long-grain rice, uncooked
- 1 teaspoon dried rosemary
- ½ teaspoon dried marjoram
- ¼ cup dried parsley, chopped
- 1 tablespoon butter or margarine
- ¼ cup onions, diced
- ½ cup slivered almonds (optional)

1. Mix together chicken bouillon cubes and water. 2. Combine all ingredients in crock pot. 3. Cook on low 4 to 6 hours, or until rice is fully cooked.

Creamy Butternut Squash Risotto

- ½ cup (1 stick) unsalted butter
- 2 tablespoons olive oil
- ½ cup finely chopped shallots (about 4 medium)
- 2 cups diced peeled and seeded butternut squash
- 1½ cups Arborio or Carnaroli rice
- ¼ cup dry white wine or vermouth
- 4¼ cups chicken broth
- ½ cup freshly grated Parmigiano-Reggiano cheese

1. Coat the insert of a 5- to 7-quart crock pot with nonstick cooking spray or line it with a slow-cooker liner according to the manufacturer's directions. 2. Heat ¼ cup of the butter with the oil in a large saucepan over medium-high heat. Add the shallots and squash and sauté until the shallots are softened, about 3 minutes. Add the rice and cook, tossing to coat with the butter, until the rice is opaque. Add the wine and cook until the wine evaporates. 3. Transfer the mixture to the slow-cooker insert and stir in the broth. Cover and cook on high for 2½ hours; check the risotto at 2 hours to make sure the broth hasn't evaporated. Stir in the remaining ¼ cup butter and ¼ cup of the cheese. 4. Serve the risotto immediately with the remaining cheese on the side.

Risotto with Gorgonzola

- ½ cup (1 stick) unsalted butter
- 2 tablespoons olive oil
- ½ cup finely chopped shallots (about 4 medium)
- 1½ cups Arborio or Carnaroli rice
- ¼ cup dry white wine or vermouth
- 4 cups chicken broth
- 1 cup crumbled Gorgonzola cheese

1. Begin by preparing the insert of a 5- to 7-quart crock pot, either by coating it with nonstick cooking spray or by lining it with a slow-cooker liner according to the manufacturer's instructions. 2. In a large saucepan over medium-high heat, melt ¼ cup of the butter together with the oil. Once the butter is melted, add the shallots and sauté them until they become soft, which should take about 4 minutes. Next, add the rice and stir it around to coat with the buttery mixture, cooking until the rice appears opaque. Afterward, pour in the wine and allow it to cook until it evaporates completely. 3. Once the wine has evaporated, transfer the entire mixture into the slow-cooker insert and stir in the broth. Cover the crock pot and set it to cook on high for 2½ hours. At the 2-hour mark, check the risotto to ensure that the broth hasn't evaporated too much. 4. When the cooking time is complete, stir in the remaining butter and the Gorgonzola cheese until well combined, and serve immediately for the best flavor and texture.

Pizza Rice

- 2 cups rice, uncooked
- 3 cups chunky pizza sauce
- 2½ cups water
- 1 (7-ounce / 170-g) can mushrooms, undrained
- 4 ounces (113 g) pepperoni, sliced
- 1 cup shredded cheese

1. In the crock pot, combine the rice, sauce, water, mushrooms, and pepperoni, stirring well to mix all the ingredients. 2. Cover the crock pot and cook on low for 10 hours or on high for 6 hours. 3. Before serving, sprinkle the dish with cheese for added flavor.

Hearty Quinoa Chicken Chili

- 1 teaspoon olive oil
- ½ yellow onion, minced
- 2 cloves garlic, minced
- 2 large boneless, skinless chicken breasts, diced
- 1 cup quinoa, rinsed
- 1 (28-ounce / 794-g) can crushed tomatoes, with the juice
- 1 (15-ounce / 425-g) can diced tomatoes with green chiles, with the juice
- 2 (15-ounce / 425-g) cans black beans, drained and rinsed
- 2 pounds (907 g) corn kernels, fresh or frozen and thawed
- 1 large bell pepper, any color, chopped
- 2½ cups chicken stock
- 1 teaspoon ground cumin
- 1 teaspoon red pepper flakes
- 1 teaspoon chili powder
- ½ teaspoon sea salt
- ½ teaspoon black pepper
- 1 (8-ounce / 227-g) container of plain Greek yogurt, for serving (optional)
- ½ cup grated Parmesan cheese, for serving (optional)

1. Heat the olive oil over medium-high heat in a medium skillet. Add the onion and garlic and sauté for 1 minute. 2. Add the chicken to the skillet and cook until browned, about 5 minutes. Put the chicken in the crock pot (see Note). 3. To the crock pot, add the quinoa, crushed tomatoes, diced tomatoes with chiles, black beans, corn, bell pepper, and chicken stock. Sprinkle in the cumin, red pepper flakes, chili powder, ½ teaspoon salt, and ½ teaspoon pepper. 4. Cover and cook on low for 5 to 7 hours. Remove the chicken, shred it, and return it to the crock pot. Season with more salt and pepper, if necessary. Keep warm until ready to serve. 5. For serving, garnish with Greek yogurt and/or Parmesan, if desired.

Cheesy Broccoli Rice Bake

- 1 cup minute rice, uncooked
- 1 (1-pound / 454-g) package frozen chopped broccoli
- 1 (8-ounce / 227-g) jar processed cheese spread
- 1 (10¾-ounce / 305-g) can cream of mushroom soup

1. Mix all ingredients together in crock pot. 2. Cover and cook on high 3 to 4 hours, or until rice and broccoli are tender but not mushy or dry.

Spicy Black Beans with Root Veggies

- 1 onion, chopped
- 1 leek, white part only, sliced
- 3 garlic cloves, minced
- 1 jalapeño pepper, minced
- 2 Yukon Gold potatoes, peeled and cubed
- 1 parsnip, peeled and cubed
- 1 carrot, sliced
- 1 cup dried black beans, sorted and rinsed
- 2 cups vegetable broth
- 2 teaspoons chili powder
- ½ teaspoon dried marjoram leaves
- ½ teaspoon salt
- ⅛ teaspoon freshly ground black pepper
- ⅛ teaspoon crushed red pepper flakes

1. In the crock pot, combine all the ingredients, ensuring everything is well mixed. 2. Cover the crock pot and cook on low for 7 to 8 hours, or until the beans and vegetables are tender. 3. Once cooked, serve and enjoy your dish.

Cheesy Grits Casserole

- 1 cup stone-ground grits
- 4½ cups chicken broth
- 4 tablespoons (½ stick) unsalted butter, melted and slightly cooled
- 2 large eggs, beaten
- ½ cup heavy cream
- 2 cup finely shredded mild Cheddar cheese

1. Apply nonstick cooking spray to the crock pot insert or line it with a slow-cooker liner, following the instructions from the manufacturer.2. In the slow-cooker, mix the grits, broth, and butter until combined. Cover and cook on low for 4 hours. After that, stir in the eggs, cream, and cheese, ensuring everything is well blended. Cover again and cook for another 4 hours until the grits become creamy and the cheese is fully melted.3. Set the slow cooker to warm and serve directly from it.

Chapter **3**

Poultry

Chapter 3 Poultry

Boneless Buffalo Chicken for Sandwiches

Prep time: 15 minutes | Cook time: 4 to 5 hours | Serves 8

- 1 cup (2 sticks) unsalted butter, melted
- ½ cup vegetable oil
- 1 cup Frank's Red Hot Hot Cayenne Pepper Sauce
- 10 chicken breast halves, skin and bones removed

1. Place the butter, oil, and hot sauce in the insert of a 5- to 7-quart slow cooker, stirring until well combined. Add the chicken, turning it to fully coat in the sauce, then layer the chicken evenly in the cooker.2. Cover and cook on low for 4 to 5 hours, making sure to turn the chicken occasionally in the sauce as it cooks. Once done, remove the chicken and shred it with two forks. Return the shredded chicken to the sauce and stir to evenly coat.3. Keep the slow cooker on warm and serve directly from it.

Slow-Cooked Duck Confit

Prep time: 15 minutes | Cook time: 6 hours | Serves 6

- ¼ cup plus 2 tablespoons coarse salt
- 4 large garlic cloves, smashed and peeled
- 4 dried bay leaves, crumbled
- 1 tablespoon juniper berries, crushed
- 1 tablespoon fresh thyme leaves
- 2 teaspoon freshly ground pepper
- 6 duck legs, untrimmed
- 6 cups duck fat, olive oil, or lard, or any combination of the three

1. In a bowl, combine salt, garlic, bay leaves, juniper berries, thyme, and pepper, rubbing spice mixture between your fingers to release aromatic oils. Generously rub onto duck legs, coating evenly. Sandwich legs in pairs, skin side out, tucking in any remaining spice mixture; cover bowl and refrigerate at least overnight or up to 2 days. 2. Preheat a 5- to 6-quart crock pot. 3. Scrape off spice mixture and rinse duck under cold water. Pat completely dry and place in the crock pot. 4. In a small saucepan over medium heat, melt duck fat and pour over duck. Cover and cook on low until oil is clear and meat is tender, 6 hours (or on high for 3 hours). Let duck cool completely in fat at room temperature, then refrigerate until ready to serve. Wipe off fat and roast at 425ºF (220ºC) just until skin is crisp and duck is heated through. (Reserve duck fat for another use.)

Slow-Cooked Chicken Jambalaya

Prep time: 30 minutes | Cook time: 5 hours | Serves 8

- 1 tablespoon olive oil
- 1 pound (454 g) skinless, boneless chicken breasts, cut into 1-inch pieces
- ¾ pound (340 g) skinless, boneless chicken thighs, cut into 1-inch pieces
- 2 large yellow onions, chopped
- 1 large green bell pepper, chopped
- 1 large stalk celery, chopped
- 2 garlic cloves, minced
- 4 ounces (113 g) turkey kielbasa, halved and cut into ¼-inch slices
- 1 (28-ounce / 794-g) can diced tomatoes, with the
- juice
- 2 cups chicken stock
- 1 teaspoon garlic powder
- 1 teaspoon paprika
- ½ teaspoon onion powder
- ½ teaspoon cayenne pepper
- ½ teaspoon dried oregano
- ½ teaspoon dried thyme
- ½ teaspoon black pepper
- ¼ teaspoon Spanish smoked paprika
- 1 cup uncooked long-grain rice
- 2 tablespoons chopped fresh flat-leaf parsley
- 1 tablespoon hot pepper sauce (like Tabasco)

1. Heat a large skillet over medium-high heat. Add the olive oil and swirl to coat. Add the chicken and cook 4 minutes, stirring occasionally. Place the chicken in crock pot. 2. In the large skillet, add the onions, bell pepper, celery, and garlic. Sauté 4 minutes or until the vegetables are tender. 3. Add the onion mixture, turkey kielbasa, tomatoes, and chicken stock to the crock pot. Sprinkle with the garlic powder, paprika, onion powder, cayenne pepper, oregano, thyme, black pepper, and Spanish smoked paprika. Cover and cook on low for 5 hours. 4. Cook the rice according to the package directions. Add the cooked rice, parsley, and hot pepper sauce to the crock pot. Cover and cook on high 15 minutes. Serve hot.

Chicken Chili Verde

- 1½ pounds (680 g) boneless, skinless chicken thighs
- 2 pounds (907 g) tomatillos, husked, cleaned, and puréed
- 1 medium onion, finely chopped
- 3 garlic cloves, minced
- ½ cup finely chopped fresh cilantro
- 2½ cups low-sodium chicken stock
- 1 tablespoon chili powder, preferably ancho
- 1 teaspoon ground cumin
- 1 teaspoon kosher salt, plus more for seasoning
- 1 (14½-ounce / 411-g) can cannellini or pinto beans, drained and rinsed
- Freshly ground black pepper
- 1 cup crushed tortilla chips, for garnish
- ½ cup sour cream, for garnish
- 1 medium red onion, finely chopped, for garnish
- 1 lime, cut into wedges, for garnish

1. Place the chicken into the slow cooker, followed by the puréed tomatillos, onion, garlic, cilantro, chicken stock, chili powder, cumin, salt, and beans. Stir everything together until well mixed. Cover the slow cooker and let it cook on low for 8 hours. 2. After cooking, use two forks to shred the chicken directly in the pot. Taste and adjust the seasoning with more salt and pepper if necessary. Spoon the mixture into bowls, then top with tortilla chips, a dollop of sour cream, red onion slices, and a squeeze of fresh lime juice.

Orange-Spiced Chicken with Sweet Potatoes

- 2 to 3 sweet potatoes, peeled and sliced
- 3 whole chicken breasts, halved
- ⅔ cup flour plus 3 tablespoons, divided
- 1 teaspoon salt
- 1 teaspoon nutmeg
- ½ teaspoon cinnamon
- Dash pepper
- Dash garlic powder
- 1 (10¾-ounce / 305-g) can cream of celery or cream of chicken soup
- 1 (4-ounce / 113-g) can sliced mushrooms, drained
- ½ cup orange juice
- ½ teaspoon grated orange rind
- 2 teaspoons brown sugar

1. Place sweet potatoes in bottom of crock pot. 2. Rinse chicken breasts and pat dry. Combine ⅔ cup flour, salt, nutmeg, cinnamon, pepper, and garlic powder. Thoroughly coat chicken in flour mixture. Place on top of sweet potatoes. 3. Combine soup with remaining ingredients. Stir well. Pour over chicken breasts. 4. Cover. Cook on low 8 to 10 hours, or on high 3 to 4 hours. 5. Serve.

Sweet and Tangy Orange Chicken

- Cooking spray or 1 tablespoon extra-virgin olive oil
- 2 garlic cloves, minced
- 1 cup orange marmalade
- ⅓ cup cornstarch
- 1 tablespoon rice vinegar
- 1½ teaspoons soy sauce
- 1 teaspoon sesame oil
- ½ teaspoon kosher salt, plus more for seasoning
- ½ teaspoon freshly ground black pepper, plus more for seasoning
- ¼ teaspoon red pepper flakes
- 2 pounds (907 g) boneless, skinless chicken breasts, cut into ½-inch pieces
- 3 cups cooked white rice, for serving
- 2 tablespoons sesame seeds, lightly toasted, for garnish

1. Use the cooking spray or olive oil to coat the inside (bottom and sides) of the crock pot. Add the garlic, marmalade, cornstarch, vinegar, soy sauce, sesame oil, salt, pepper, and red pepper flakes and whisk to combine. Add the chicken and stir to coat. Cover and cook on low for 4 hours. 2. Season with additional salt and pepper, as needed. Scoop the rice onto individual plates, spoon the chicken on top, garnish with the sesame seeds and serve immediately.

Pesto Chicken with Rustic Stewed Vegetables

- 1 zucchini, cut into 1-inch pieces
- 1 cup grape tomatoes
- 1 red bell pepper, cored and sliced thin
- ½ red onion, halved and sliced thin
- 1 tablespoon assorted fresh herbs
- 1 teaspoon extra-virgin olive oil
- ⅛ teaspoon sea salt
- Freshly ground black pepper
- 2 bone-in, skinless chicken thighs, about 8 ounces (227 g) each
- ¼ cup pesto

1. Put the zucchini, grape tomatoes, red bell pepper, onion, and herbs in the crock pot and gently stir until mixed together. Drizzle the vegetables with the olive oil. Season with the salt and a few grinds of the black pepper. 2. In a medium bowl, coat the chicken on all sides with the pesto, then place the chicken on top of the vegetables. 3. Cover and cook on low for 6 to 8 hours until the vegetables are very tender and the chicken is cooked through.

Gran's Big Potluck

- 2½ to 3 pounds (1.1 to 1.4 kg) stewing hen, cut into pieces
- ½ pound (227 g) stewing beef, cubed
- 1 (½-pound / 227-g) veal shoulder or roast, cubed
- 1½ quarts water
- ½ pound (227 g) small red potatoes, cubed
- ½ pound (227 g) small onions, cut in half
- 1 cup sliced carrots
- 1 cup chopped celery
- 1 green pepper, chopped
- 1 (1-pound / 454-g) package frozen lima beans
- 1 cup fresh or frozen okra
- 1 cup whole-kernel corn
- 1 (8-ounce / 227-g) can whole tomatoes with juice
- 1 (15-ounce / 425-g) can tomato purée
- 1 teaspoon salt
- ¼ to ½ teaspoon pepper
- 1 teaspoon dry mustard
- ½ teaspoon chili powder
- ¼ cup chopped fresh parsley

1. Place all ingredients, except for the final 5 seasonings, into a large crock pot or divide between two medium-sized ones if needed. Mix everything together to combine. 2. Cover the crock pot and cook on low for 10 to 12 hours, allowing the flavors to develop. 3. In the last hour of cooking, stir in the remaining seasonings and let them blend into the dish.

Slow-Cooked Punjabi Chicken Curry

- 2 tablespoons vegetable oil
- 3 onions, finely diced
- 6 garlic cloves, finely chopped
- 1 heaped tablespoon freshly grated ginger
- 1 (14-ounce / 397-g) can plum tomatoes
- 1 teaspoon salt
- 1 teaspoon turmeric
- 1 teaspoon chili powder
- Handful coriander stems, finely chopped
- 3 fresh green chiles, finely chopped
- 12 pieces chicken, mixed thighs and drumsticks, or a whole chicken, skinned, trimmed, and chopped
- 2 teaspoons garam masala
- Handful fresh coriander leaves, chopped

1. Heat the oil in a frying pan (or in the crock pot if you have a sear setting). Add the diced onions and cook for 5 minutes. Add the garlic and continue to cook for 10 minutes until the onions are brown. 2. Heat the crock pot to high and add the onion-and-garlic mixture. Stir in the ginger, tomatoes, salt, turmeric, chili powder, coriander stems, and chiles. 3. Add the chicken pieces. Cover and cook on low for 6 hours, or on high for 4 hours. 4. Once

cooked, check the seasoning, and then stir in the garam masala and coriander leaves.

Chicken and Sausage Cacciatore

- 1 large green pepper, sliced in 1-inch strips
- 1 cup sliced mushrooms
- 1 medium onion, sliced in rings
- 1 pound (454 g) skinless, boneless chicken breasts, browned
- 1 pound (454 g) Italian sausage, browned
- ½ teaspoon dried oregano
- ½ teaspoon dried basil
- 1½ cups Italian-style tomato sauce

1. Place the vegetables in an even layer at the bottom of the crock pot. 2. Add the meat on top of the vegetables, making sure it is evenly distributed. 3. Sprinkle oregano and basil over the meat for seasoning. 4. Pour the tomato sauce evenly over the top. 5. Cover the crock pot and cook on low for 8 hours, letting the flavors meld together. 6. For the last 30 minutes, remove the lid to allow the sauce to reduce and thicken. 7. Once done, serve hot and enjoy.

Dad's Hearty Spicy Chicken Curry

- 4 pounds (1.8 kg) chicken pieces, with bones
- Water
- 2 onions, diced
- 1 (10-ounce / 283-g) package frozen chopped spinach, thawed and squeezed dry
- 1 cup plain yogurt
- 2 to 3 diced red potatoes
- 3 teaspoons salt
- 1 teaspoon garlic powder
- 1 teaspoon ground ginger
- 1 teaspoon ground cumin
- 1 teaspoon ground coriander
- 1 teaspoon pepper
- 1 teaspoon ground cloves
- 1 teaspoon ground cardamom
- 1 teaspoon ground cinnamon
- ½ teaspoon chili powder
- 1 teaspoon red pepper flakes
- 3 teaspoons turmeric

1. Place chicken in large crock pot. Cover with water. 2. Cover. Cook on high 2 hours, or until tender. 3. Drain chicken. Remove from crock pot. Cool briefly and cut/shred into small pieces. Return to crock pot. 4. Add remaining ingredients. 5. Cover. Cook on low 4 to 6 hours, or until potatoes are tender. 6. Serve.

Sauerkraut and Turkey Sausage

Prep time: 5 minutes | Cook time: 4 to 6 hours | Serves 8

- 1 large can sauerkraut
- ¼ to ½ cup brown sugar, according to your taste

preference
- 1 (8-inch) link spicy or smoked turkey sausage

1. Add the sauerkraut to the crock pot, spreading it out evenly.2. Sprinkle the brown sugar over the sauerkraut to add sweetness.3. Slice the turkey sausage into ¼-inch rounds and place them on top of the sauerkraut.4. Cover and cook on low for 4 to 6 hours, allowing the flavors to blend together.

Tropical Maui Pineapple Chicken

Prep time: 20 minutes | Cook time: 4 to 6 hours | Serves 6

- 6 boneless chicken breast halves
- 2 tablespoons oil
- 1 (14½-ounce / 411-g) can chicken broth
- 1 (20-ounce / 567-g) pineapple chunks
- ¼ cup vinegar
- 2 tablespoons brown sugar
- 2 teaspoons soy sauce
- 1 garlic clove, minced
- 1 medium green bell pepper, chopped
- 3 tablespoons cornstarch
- ¼ cup water

1. Brown chicken in oil. Transfer chicken to crock pot. 2. Combine remaining ingredients. Pour over chicken. 3. Cover. Cook on high 4 to 6 hours. 4. Serve.

Barbecued Turkey

Prep time: 15 minutes | Cook time: 3 to 4 hours | Serves 6

- 3 large onions, coarsely chopped
- 2 red bell peppers, seeded and coarsely chopped
- 1 (4-pound / 1.8-kg) bone-in turkey breast, skin removed
- 1 cup ketchup
- 1 cup tomato sauce
- ½ cup Dijon mustard
- ¼ cup firmly packed light brown sugar
- 2 tablespoons Worcestershire sauce
- ½ teaspoon Tabasco sauce

1. Place the onions and bell peppers evenly at the bottom of a 5- to 7-quart slow cooker. Lay the turkey breast on top of the vegetables. In a small bowl, mix together the ketchup, tomato sauce, mustard, sugar, Worcestershire sauce, and Tabasco until well combined.2. Brush a portion of the barbecue sauce onto the turkey breast, then pour the remaining sauce into the slow cooker. Cover and cook on high for 3 to 4 hours, or until the turkey reaches an internal temperature of 175°F (79°C) using an instant-read thermometer.3. Once cooked, carefully lift the turkey out of the slow cooker, cover it with aluminum foil, and let it rest for 20 minutes before slicing.4. Strain the sauce through a fine-mesh sieve into a bowl, discarding any solids. Return the strained sauce to the slow cooker.5. Slice the turkey and either serve it with the sauce on the side or return the sliced turkey to the slow cooker with the sauce to keep warm and serve directly from the cooker.

Bacon-Mushroom Chicken

Prep time: 15 minutes | Cook time: 7 to 8 hours | Serves 8

- 3 tablespoons coconut oil, divided
- ¼ pound (113 g) bacon, diced
- 2 pounds (907 g) chicken (breasts, thighs, drumsticks)
- 2 cups quartered button
- mushrooms
- 1 sweet onion, diced
- 1 tablespoon minced garlic
- ½ cup chicken broth
- 2 teaspoons chopped thyme
- 1 cup coconut cream

1. Grease the crock pot insert with 1 tablespoon of coconut oil.2. Heat the remaining 2 tablespoons of coconut oil in a large skillet over medium-high heat.3. Add the bacon to the skillet and cook until crispy, about 5 minutes. Remove the bacon with a slotted spoon and set it aside on a plate.4. Place the chicken in the same skillet, browning each side for about 5 minutes.5. Transfer the browned chicken and cooked bacon into the crock pot, then add the mushrooms, onion, garlic, broth, and thyme.6. Cover and cook on low for 7 to 8 hours until the chicken is tender.7. Stir in the coconut cream just before serving, and enjoy.

Creamy Chicken Curry

Prep time: 20 minutes | Cook time: 2 to 4 hours | Serves 4 to 6

- 2 (10¾-ounce / 305-g) cans cream of mushroom soup
- 1 soup can water
- 2 teaspoons curry powder
- ⅓ to ½ cup chopped almonds, toasted
- 4 skinless chicken breast halves, cooked and cubed

1. Add all ingredients to the crock pot and mix well to ensure even distribution.2. Cover and cook on low for 2 to 4 hours, stirring occasionally to prevent sticking and ensure thorough cooking.3. Once ready, dish out and serve immediately.

Saucy Turkey Breast

Prep time: 5 minutes | Cook time: 1 to 5 hours | Serves 6 to 8

- 1 (3- to 5-pound / 1.4- to 2.3-kg) bone-in or boneless turkey breast
- 1 envelope dry onion soup mix
- Salt and pepper to taste
- 1 (16-ounce / 454-g) can cranberry sauce, jellied or whole-berry
- 2 tablespoons cornstarch
- 2 tablespoons cold water

1. Season both sides of the turkey breast with salt, pepper, and the soup mix. Place the seasoned turkey breast into the crock pot.2. Spoon the cranberry sauce over the top of the turkey breast, spreading it evenly.3. Cover the crock pot and cook on low for 4 to 5 hours or on high for 1 to 3 hours, or until the turkey is tender but not overcooked. Ensure the internal temperature reaches 180ºF (82ºC) using a meat thermometer.4. Once done, carefully remove the turkey from the crock pot and let it rest for 10 minutes while keeping the sauce in the cooker.5. While the turkey rests, turn the cooker to high. In a small bowl, whisk together the cornstarch and cold water until smooth. Once the sauce in the cooker starts to boil, stir in the cornstarch mixture. Let it simmer until the sauce thickens.6. Slice the turkey breast and serve with the thickened sauce drizzled over the top.

Marinated Chinese Chicken Salad

Prep time: 25 minutes | Cook time: 3 to 8 hours | Serves 8

Marinade:

- 3 cloves minced garlic
- 1 tablespoon fresh ginger, grated
- 1 teaspoon dried red pepper flakes

Dressing:

- ½ cup rice wine vinegar
- 1 clove garlic, minced

Salad:

- 1 large head iceberg lettuce, shredded
- 2 carrots, julienned
- ½ cup chopped roasted

- 2 tablespoons honey
- 3 tablespoons low-sodium soy sauce
- 6 boneless, skinless chicken breast halves

- 1 teaspoon fresh grated ginger
- 1 tablespoon honey

  peanuts
- ¼ cup chopped cilantro
- ½ package mei fun noodles, fried in hot oil

1. In a small bowl, whisk together all the marinade ingredients until well combined.2. Place the chicken in the crock pot and pour the marinade over it, ensuring each piece is thoroughly coated.3. Cover and cook on low for 6 to 8 hours, or on high for 3 to 4 hours, until the chicken is tender.4. Once cooked, remove the chicken from the crock pot and allow it to cool slightly. Reserve the cooking juices. Shred the chicken into bite-sized pieces.5. In a separate small bowl, mix the dressing ingredients together with ½ cup of the reserved crock pot juices.6. In a large serving bowl, toss together the shredded chicken, lettuce, carrots, peanuts, cilantro, and noodles until evenly distributed.7. Just before serving, drizzle the prepared salad dressing over the mixture. Toss everything well and serve immediately.

Hearty Chicken and Shrimp Jambalaya

Prep time: 15 minutes | Cook time: 2¼ to 3¾ hours | Serves 5 to 6

- 1 (3½- to 4-pound / 1.6- to 1.8-kg) roasting chicken, cut up
- 3 onions, diced
- 1 carrot, sliced
- 3 to 4 garlic cloves, minced
- 1 teaspoon dried oregano
- 1 teaspoon dried basil
- 1 teaspoon salt
- ⅛ teaspoon white pepper
- 1 (14-ounce / 397-g) crushed tomatoes
- 1 pound (454 g) shelled raw shrimp
- 2 cups rice, cooked

1. Combine all ingredients except shrimp and rice in crock pot. 2. Cover. Cook on low 2 to 3½ hours, or until chicken is tender. 3. Add shrimp and rice. 4. Cover. Cook on high 15 to 20 minutes, or until shrimp are done.

Zesty Garlic-Lime Chicken

Prep time: 10 minutes | Cook time: 4 to 8 hours | Serves 5

- 5 chicken breast halves
- ½ cup soy sauce
- ¼ to ⅓ cup lime juice, according to your taste preference
- 1 tablespoon Worcestershire
- sauce
- 2 garlic cloves, minced, or 1 teaspoon garlic powder
- ½ teaspoon dry mustard
- ½ teaspoon ground pepper

1. Place chicken in crock pot. 2. Combine remaining ingredients and pour over chicken. 3. Cover. Cook on high 4 to 6 hours, or on low 6 to 8 hours.

Creamy Tarragon Chicken Delight

- 3 whole chicken breasts, skin removed and halved
- 1 (10¾-ounce / 305-g) can low-sodium condensed cream of chicken soup
- ½ cup cooking sherry
- 1 (4-ounce / 113-g) can
- sliced mushrooms, drained
- 1 teaspoon Worcestershire sauce
- 1 teaspoon dried tarragon leaves or dried rosemary
- ¼ teaspoon garlic powder

1. Rinse chicken breasts and pat dry. Place in crock pot. 2. Combine remaining ingredients and pour over chicken breasts, making sure that all pieces are glazed with the sauce. 3. Cover and cook on low 8 to 10 hours, or on high 4 to 5 hours. 4. Serve.

Spicy Asian Braised Napa Cabbage Wraps

- 1 head Napa cabbage
- 2 cups chicken broth
- ½ cup soy sauce
- 4 slices fresh ginger
- 2 tablespoons vegetable oil
- 2 cloves garlic, minced
- 1 teaspoon freshly grated ginger
- 6 canned water chestnuts, finely chopped
- 2 chicken breast halves, skin and bones removed, finely chopped
- 4 green onions, finely chopped, using the white and tender green parts
- 2 tablespoons hoisin sauce
- 1 tablespoon cornstarch mixed with 2 tablespoons water

1. Core the cabbage and gently separate the leaves, being careful to avoid tearing them. In a large stockpot, bring the broth, soy sauce, and ginger to a boil.2. Blanch each cabbage leaf individually for about 30 seconds until soft and pliable. Drain the leaves and set aside. Pour the broth mixture into the insert of a 5- to 7-quart crock pot, cover, and set it to warm while you prepare the filling.3. Heat oil in a sauté pan over high heat. Add the garlic, ginger, and water chestnuts, sautéing for 30 seconds. Add the chicken and cook until it turns white, about 3 to 5 minutes.4. Transfer the cooked mixture to a bowl and stir in the green onions and hoisin sauce. Take a cabbage leaf and place 2 to 3 tablespoons of the filling at the stem end, then roll it up, tucking in the sides as you roll. Arrange the cabbage rolls on a rack in the crock pot.5. Cover and cook on high for 1½ to 2 hours, or until the chicken is fully cooked. Remove the cabbage rolls and set them aside. Strain the broth through a fine-mesh sieve into a saucepan, bring it to a boil, then stir in the

cornstarch mixture and bring it back to a boil until thickened.6. Serve the cabbage wraps with the sauce on the side for dipping.

Hearty Mulligan Chicken Stew

- 1 (3-pound / 1.4-kg) stewing hen, cut up, or 4 pounds (1.8 kg) chicken legs and thighs
- 1½ teaspoons salt
- 1 (¼-pound / 113-g) salt pork or bacon, cut in 1-inch squares
- 4 cups tomatoes, peeled and sliced
- 2 cups fresh corn, or 1
- (1-pound / 454-g) package frozen corn
- 1 cup coarsely chopped potatoes
- 1 (10-ounce / 283-g) package lima beans, frozen
- ½ cup chopped onions
- 1 teaspoon salt
- ¼ teaspoon pepper
- Dash of cayenne pepper

1. Place chicken in very large crock pot. Add water to cover. Add 1½ teaspoons salt. 2. Cover. Cook on low 2 hours. Add more water if needed. 3. Add remaining ingredients. (If you don't have a large cooker, divide the stew between 2 average-sized ones.) Simmer on low 5 hours longer.

Jerk Chicken

- ½ cup extra-virgin olive oil, divided
- 2 pounds (907 g) boneless chicken (breast and thighs)
- 1 sweet onion, quartered
- 4 garlic cloves
- 2 scallions, white and green parts, coarsely chopped
- 2 habanero chiles, stemmed and seeded
- 2 tablespoons granulated erythritol
- 1 tablespoon grated fresh ginger
- 2 teaspoons allspice
- 1 teaspoon dried thyme
- ½ teaspoon cardamom
- ½ teaspoon salt
- 2 tablespoons chopped cilantro, for garnish

1. Lightly coat the crock pot insert with 1 tablespoon of olive oil.2. Place the chicken pieces in an even layer at the bottom of the crock pot.3. In a blender, combine the remaining olive oil, onion, garlic, scallions, chiles, erythritol, ginger, allspice, thyme, cardamom, and salt. Blend until you get a thick, smooth sauce.4. Pour the sauce over the chicken, making sure each piece is well coated by turning them in the sauce.5. Cover and cook on low for 7 to 8 hours until the chicken is tender and fully cooked.6. Serve the chicken topped with fresh cilantro for a bright, flavorful finish.

Creamy Tarragon Chicken with Mushrooms

Prep time: 25 minutes | Cook time: 3 to 5½ hours | Serves 6

- 2 tablespoons extra-virgin olive oil
- 8 chicken breast halves, skin and bones removed
- Salt and freshly ground black pepper
- 1 clove garlic, minced
- 1 medium onion, finely chopped
- 1 pound (454 g) white button mushrooms, halved
- or quartered if large
- 1 teaspoon dried tarragon
- ¼ cup dry white wine or vermouth
- 1½ cups chicken broth
- ¼ cup Dijon mustard
- ½ cup heavy cream
- 2 teaspoons cornstarch
- 2 tablespoons finely chopped fresh tarragon, plus additional for garnish

1. Heat the oil in a large skillet over high heat. Sprinkle the chicken evenly with 1 teaspoon salt and ½ teaspoon pepper. Add the chicken to the skillet and brown on all sides. Transfer the chicken to the insert of a 5- to 7-quart crock pot. 2. Add the garlic, onion, mushrooms, and dried tarragon to the skillet and sauté until the onion is softened and the mushroom liquid has evaporated, 7 to 10 minutes. Deglaze the skillet with the wine, scraping up any browned bits from the bottom. 3. Transfer the contents of the skillet to the slow-cooker insert. Add the broth and mustard to the cooker and stir to combine. Cover the crock pot and cook on high for 2½ hours or on low for 4 to 5 hours. 4. Add cream, cornstarch, and two tablespoons fresh tarragon to the crock pot and stir to combine. Cover and cook for an additional 15 minutes on high or 30 minutes on low, until the sauce is thickened. Season with salt and pepper. 5. Serve the chicken garnished with the additional fresh tarragon.

Barbecued Chicken Legs

Prep time: 15 minutes | Cook time: 8 hours | Serves 8

- 10 chicken legs, skin removed
- 1 teaspoon salt
- ½ teaspoon freshly ground black pepper
- 2 tablespoons unsalted butter
- 1 medium onion, finely chopped
- 1 clove garlic, minced
- 1 tablespoon Dijon mustard
- 1 tablespoon Worcestershire sauce
- 1½ cups ketchup
- ½ cup chicken broth
- ½ cup firmly packed light brown sugar
- ¼ cup molasses
- ½ teaspoon hot sauce

1. Lightly spray the insert of a 5- to 7-quart crock pot with nonstick cooking spray or use a slow-cooker liner according to the manufacturer's instructions.2. Season the chicken legs evenly with salt and pepper, then place them in the crock pot.3. In a large saucepan over medium-high heat, melt the butter. Add the onion and garlic, sautéing for about 3 minutes until the onion softens.4. Stir in the remaining ingredients and mix well. Pour this sauce over the chicken in the crock pot.5. Cover and cook on low for 8 hours until the chicken is tender and fully cooked. Once done, remove the lid and skim off any excess fat.6. Serve the chicken directly from the crock pot set to warm, ensuring it's well coated with the sauce.

Fruited Barbecue Chicken

Prep time: 5 minutes | Cook time: 4 hours | Serves 6 to 8

- 1 (29-ounce / 822-g) can tomato sauce
- 1 (20-ounce / 567-g) unsweetened crushed pineapple, undrained
- 2 tablespoons brown sugar
- 3 tablespoons vinegar
- 1 tablespoon instant minced onion
- 1 teaspoon paprika
- 2 teaspoons Worcestershire sauce
- ¼ teaspoon garlic powder
- ⅛ teaspoon pepper
- 3 pounds (1.4 kg) chicken, skinned and cubed
- 1 (11-ounce / 312-g) can mandarin oranges, drained

1. Mix together all ingredients except the chicken and oranges in the crock pot. Then add the chicken pieces, making sure they are fully coated.2. Cover the crock pot and cook on high for 4 hours, allowing the flavors to meld as the chicken cooks through.3. Right before serving, gently stir in the orange slices to combine. Serve immediately and enjoy.

Tropical Chicken à la Fruit

Prep time: 20 minutes | Cook time: 6 to 8 hours | Serves 5 to 6

- ½ cup crushed pineapple, drained
- 3 whole peaches, mashed
- 2 tablespoons lemon juice
- 2 tablespoons soy sauce
- ½ to ¾ teaspoon salt
- ¼ teaspoon pepper
- 1 chicken, cut up
- Nonstick cooking spray

1. Spray crock pot with nonstick cooking spray. 2. Mix pineapple, peaches, lemon juice, soy sauce, and salt and pepper in a large bowl. 3. Dip chicken pieces in sauce and then place in crock pot. Pour remaining sauce over all. 4. Cover and cook on low 6 to 8 hours, or until chicken is tender but not dry.

Tomato Chicken Curry

Prep time: 30 minutes | Cook time: 2 to 6 hours | Serves 6 to 8

- 1 (28-ounce / 794-g) can tomatoes
- 4 whole chicken breasts, cut in half
- 1 onion, chopped
- Half a green pepper, chopped
- 2 carrots, chopped
- 2 ribs celery, chopped
- 1 to 2 tablespoons curry
- 1 teaspoon turmeric
- ½ teaspoon salt
- ¼ teaspoon pepper
- 1 tablespoon sugar
- 1 chicken bouillon cube dissolved in ¼ cup hot water

1. Add all the ingredients to the crock pot, ensuring everything is well combined.2. Cover the crock pot and cook on high for 2 to 3 hours, or on low for 5 to 6 hours, until everything is fully cooked and flavors are blended. Serve hot.

Thai Peanut Wings

Prep time: 20 minutes | Cook time: 3 hours | Serves 8

- 3 pounds (1.4 kg) chicken wing drumettes
- ¼ cup olive oil
- 1½ teaspoons salt
- 1 teaspoon sweet paprika
- Freshly ground black pepper
- Sauce:
- 1 (14-ounce / 397-g) can coconut milk
- ½ cup chicken broth
- 1 cup smooth peanut butter
- ¼ cup firmly packed brown sugar
- 2 tablespoons soy sauce
- 2 teaspoons freshly grated ginger
- ¼ teaspoon hot sauce
- ½ cup finely chopped fresh cilantro, for garnish
- ½ cup finely chopped roasted peanuts, for garnish

1. Spray the insert of a 5- to 7-quart crock pot with nonstick cooking spray and preheat the broiler for 10 minutes.2. In a large bowl, toss the wings with olive oil, salt, paprika, and freshly ground pepper until evenly coated. Arrange the wings on a wire rack placed over a baking sheet and broil for about 5 minutes until crispy on one side.3. Flip the wings and broil for another 5 minutes until the other side is crispy and browned.4. Remove the wings from the oven. If preparing ahead, let them cool and refrigerate for up to 2 days. Otherwise, transfer the wings directly to the crock pot insert.5. In a small saucepan over medium heat, mix together all the sauce ingredients, stirring frequently.6. Heat the sauce until it starts to boil, then pour it over the wings, turning them to coat evenly.7. Cover the crock pot and cook on high for 3 hours, turning the wings occasionally to ensure they're well coated in the sauce.8. Once done, garnish the wings with cilantro and peanuts, and serve directly from the slow cooker set to warm.

Sweet and Spicy Chicken

Prep time: 10 minutes | Cook time: 3½ hours | Serves 6

- 2 teaspoons ground cumin
- ½ teaspoon ground cinnamon
- ¾ teaspoon coarse sea salt
- ½ teaspoon black pepper
- 4 chicken leg quarters
- 1 tablespoon extra-virgin olive oil
- 1 medium yellow onion, cut
- into ½-inch wedges (root end left intact)
- 3 garlic cloves, minced
- 1 (3-inch) piece fresh peeled ginger, sliced into rounds
- 1 (28-ounce / 794-g) can diced tomatoes, with the juice
- ½ cup raisins

1. In a large resealable plastic bag, mix together the cumin, cinnamon, salt, and black pepper. Add the chicken to the bag, seal it, and shake until the chicken is evenly coated with the spices.2. Heat olive oil in a large skillet over medium-high heat. Place the chicken in the skillet, skin-side down, and cook until golden brown, about 4 minutes. Flip the chicken and cook for an additional 2 minutes.3. In the crock pot, layer the onion, garlic, and ginger at the bottom.4. Place the browned chicken, skin-side up, on top of the onion mixture in the crock pot. Pour the tomatoes and sprinkle the raisins over the chicken.5. Cover the crock pot and cook until the chicken is tender—about 3½ hours on high or 6 hours on low. Serve the dish hot and enjoy.

Savory Herbed Chicken and Stuffing Casserole

Prep time: 20 minutes | Cook time: 4½ to 5 hours | Serves 14 to 16

- 2½ cups chicken broth
- 1 cup butter, melted
- ½ cup chopped onions
- ½ cup chopped celery
- 1 (4-ounce / 113-g) can mushrooms, stems and pieces, drained
- ¼ cup dried parsley flakes
- 1½ teaspoons rubbed sage
- 1 teaspoon poultry
- seasoning
- 1 teaspoon salt
- ½ teaspoon pepper
- 12 cups day-old bread cubes (½-inch pieces)
- 2 eggs
- 1 (10¾-ounce / 305-g) can cream of chicken soup
- 5 to 6 cups cubed cooked chicken

1. Combine all ingredients except bread, eggs, soup, and chicken in saucepan. Simmer for 10 minutes. 2. Place bread cubes in large bowl. 3. Combine eggs and soup. Stir into broth mixture until smooth. Pour over bread and toss well. 4. Layer half of stuffing and then half of chicken into very large crock pot (or two medium-sized cookers). Repeat layers. 5. Cover. Cook on low 4½ to 5 hours.

Chicken and Mushroom Farro Risotto

Prep time: 15 minutes | Cook time: 4 to 7 hours | Serves 4

- 2¼ cups chicken stock
- 1 cup whole farro
- 1 pound (454 g) cremini or button mushrooms, halved, or quartered if large
- 2 leeks, white and light green parts only, halved, sliced, and rinsed
- 1 bay leaf
- ¼ teaspoon ground nutmeg
- 1¼ teaspoons sea salt
- ¼ teaspoon black pepper
- 4 small boneless, skinless chicken thighs (about 1 pound / 454 g)
- 1 (3-inch) piece Parmesan cheese rind
- ⅓ cup grated Parmesan, plus more for serving (optional)
- 2 tablespoons unsalted butter, cut into pieces, for serving (optional)
- ¼ cup chopped fresh flat-leaf parsley, for serving (optional)

1. Combine the stock, farro, mushrooms, leeks, and Parmesan rind in the crock pot. Add the bay leaf and nutmeg, 1¼ teaspoons salt, and ¼ teaspoon pepper. 2. Arrange the chicken atop the other contents in the crock pot. Cover and cook until the chicken is tender, on low for 6 to 7 hours or on high for 4 to 5 hours. 3. To serve, discard the Parmesan rind and bay leaf. Shred the chicken into large pieces and return to the risotto. Stir in the grated Parmesan cheese. Stir in the butter, if using. 4. Sprinkle the risotto with the parsley, if desired, and serve hot with additional grated Parmesan, if desired.

Hearty Italian Chicken and Bean Stew

Prep time: 20 minutes | Cook time: 3 to 6 hours | Serves 4

- 2 boneless, skinless chicken breast halves, uncooked, cut in 1½-inch pieces
- 1 (19-ounce / 539-g) can cannellini beans, drained and rinsed
- 1 (15½-ounce / 439-g) can kidney beans, drained and rinsed
- 1 (14½-ounce / 411-g) can low-sodium diced tomatoes, undrained
- 1 cup chopped celery
- 1 cup sliced carrots
- 2 small garlic cloves, coarsely chopped
- 1 cup water
- ½ cup dry red wine or low-fat chicken broth
- 3 tablespoons tomato paste
- 1 tablespoon sugar
- 1½ teaspoons dried Italian seasoning

1. Combine chicken, cannellini beans, kidney beans, tomatoes, celery, carrots, and garlic in crock pot. Mix well. 2. In medium bowl, combine all remaining ingredients. Mix well. Pour over chicken and vegetables. Mix well. 3. Cover. Cook on low 5 to 6 hours, or on high 3 hours.

Chicken and Shrimp Rice Casserole

Prep time: 20 minutes | Cook time: 3 to 8 hours | Serves 6

- 1¼ cups rice, uncooked
- 2 tablespoons butter, melted
- 3 cups fat-free, low-sodium chicken broth
- 1 cup water
- 3 cups cut-up, cooked skinless chicken breast
- 2 (4-ounce / 113-g) cans
- sliced mushrooms, drained
- ⅓ cup light soy sauce
- 1 (12-ounce / 340-g) package shelled frozen shrimp
- 8 green onions, chopped, 2 tablespoons reserved
- ⅔ cup slivered almonds

1. Combine rice and butter in crock pot. Stir to coat rice well. 2. Add remaining ingredients except almonds and 2 tablespoons green onions. 3. Cover. Cook on low 6 to 8 hours, or on high 3 to 4 hours, until rice is tender. 4. Sprinkle almonds and green onions over top before serving.

Lemon Garlic Braised Chicken Thighs

Prep time: 15 minutes | Cook time: 7 to 8 hours | Serves 4

- ¼ cup extra-virgin olive oil, divided
- 1½ pounds (680 g) boneless chicken thighs
- 1 teaspoon paprika
- Salt, for seasoning
- Freshly ground black
- pepper, for seasoning
- 1 sweet onion, chopped
- 4 garlic cloves, thinly sliced
- ½ cup chicken broth
- 2 tablespoons freshly squeezed lemon juice
- ½ cup Greek yogurt

1. Lightly grease the insert of the crock pot with 1 tablespoon of the olive oil. 2. Season the thighs with paprika, salt, and pepper. 3. In a large skillet over medium-high heat, heat the remaining olive oil. Add the chicken and brown for 5 minutes, turning once. 4. Transfer the chicken to the insert and add the onion, garlic, broth, and lemon juice. 5. Cover and cook on low for 7 to 8 hours. 6. Stir in the yogurt and serve.

Thyme Turkey Legs

Prep time: 15 minutes | Cook time: 7 to 8 hours | Serves 6

- 3 tablespoons extra-virgin olive oil, divided
- 2 pounds (907 g) boneless turkey legs
- Salt, for seasoning
- Freshly ground black pepper, for seasoning
- 1 tablespoon dried thyme
- 2 teaspoons poultry seasoning
- ½ cup chicken broth
- 2 tablespoons chopped fresh parsley, for garnish

1. Lightly coat the crock pot insert with 1 tablespoon of olive oil.2. In a large skillet over medium-high heat, heat the remaining 2 tablespoons of olive oil.3. Season the turkey generously with salt, pepper, thyme, and poultry seasoning. Place the turkey in the skillet and brown it for about 7 minutes, turning once to ensure even browning.4. Transfer the browned turkey to the crock pot and pour in the broth.5. Cover the crock pot and cook on low for 7 to 8 hours, until the turkey is tender and fully cooked.6. Before serving, sprinkle the turkey with fresh parsley for garnish. Enjoy it hot.

Duck Carnitas Tacos

Prep time: 15 minutes | Cook time: 6 hours | Serves 6 to 8

- ½ cup fresh tangerine juice (or orange juice)
- 2 tablespoons fresh lime juice, plus lime wedges for serving
- 2 chipotle chiles in adobo sauce, finely chopped
- 2 garlic cloves, minced
- 1½ teaspoons coarse salt
- 6 duck legs
- Warm tortillas, chopped avocado, chopped radishes, toasted pepitas, and cilantro, for serving

1. Preheat a 5- to 6-quart crock pot.2. In the crock pot, combine the tangerine juice, lime juice, chipotles, garlic, and salt, stirring until everything is well mixed. Place the duck in the crock pot, skin side up. Cover and cook on low for 6 hours, or on high for 3 hours, until the duck is tender.3. Once the duck is done, transfer it to a platter and let it cool slightly. Remove the skin, and shred the meat from the bones into large pieces. Pour the cooking juices into a heatproof bowl, and skim off the fat into a separate bowl.4. In a large nonstick skillet, heat ¼ cup of the reserved duck fat over high heat. Add the shredded duck and cook, stirring frequently, until crispy, about 6 to 7 minutes. Stir in a few tablespoons of the reserved cooking juices for extra flavor.5. Serve the crispy duck immediately with tortillas, avocado slices, radishes, pepitas, and fresh cilantro.

Ginger-Soy Pacific Chicken Thighs

Prep time: 10 minutes | Cook time: 7 to 8 hours | Serves 6

- 6 to 8 skinless chicken thighs
- ½ cup soy sauce
- 2 tablespoons brown sugar
- 2 tablespoons grated fresh ginger
- 2 garlic cloves, minced

1. Wash and dry chicken. Place in crock pot. 2. Combine remaining ingredients. Pour over chicken. 3. Cover. Cook on high 1 hour. Reduce heat to low and cook 6 to 7 hours. 4. Serve.

Sweet Aromatic Chicken

Prep time: 5 minutes | Cook time: 5 to 6 hours | Serves 6 to 8

- ½ cup coconut milk
- ½ cup water
- 8 chicken thighs, skinned
- ½ cup brown sugar
- 2 tablespoons soy sauce
- ⅛ teaspoon ground cloves
- 2 garlic cloves, minced

1. Mix the coconut milk and water together, then pour the mixture into a greased crock pot.2. Add the remaining ingredients in the order they are listed, layering them evenly.3. Cover the crock pot and cook on low for 5 to 6 hours, until everything is fully cooked and tender. Serve warm.

Chapter 4

Beef, Pork, and Lamb

Chapter 4 Beef, Pork, and Lamb

Creamy Beef Risotto

Prep time: 20 minutes | Cook time: 5 hours | Serves 2

- ½ pound (227 g) lean ground beef
- 1½ cups Arborio rice
- 1 onion, chopped
- 2 garlic cloves, minced
- ¼ cup dry white wine
- 4 cups beef stock
- ½ teaspoon salt
- ⅛ teaspoon freshly ground black pepper
- ½ cup grated Parmesan cheese
- 1 tablespoon butter

1. In a medium skillet over medium heat, cook the ground beef, stirring to break up the meat, until browned, about 10 minutes. Add the rice and cook for 2 to 3 minutes, stirring constantly, until the rice is toasted. Drain off excess fat. 2. In the crock pot, combine the beef mixture, onion, and garlic. Add the wine, stock, salt, and pepper and stir well. 3. Cover and cook on low for 5 hours. 4. Stir in the cheese and butter, let stand for 5 minutes, and serve.

Maple Bourbon Pork Chops

Prep time: 15 minutes | Cook time: 3 to 8 hours | Serves 6

- 2 tablespoons olive oil
- 1½ teaspoons salt
- ½ teaspoon freshly ground black pepper
- 6 (1-inch-thick) pork loin chops
- 2 tablespoons unsalted butter
- 2 medium onions, finely chopped
- ½ cup ketchup
- ½ cup bourbon
- ¼ cup pure maple syrup
- 1 teaspoon Tabasco sauce
- 1 teaspoon dry mustard
- ½ cup beef broth

1. In a large skillet, heat the oil over high heat. Season the pork chops evenly with salt and pepper, then add them to the skillet.2. Brown the pork chops on both sides, working in batches to avoid overcrowding the pan. Once browned, transfer the pork chops to the insert of a 5- to 7-quart crock pot.3. Reduce the skillet heat to medium-high and melt the butter. Add the onions and sauté for about 5 minutes until they start to soften. Add the remaining ingredients to the skillet, scraping up any browned bits from the bottom of the pan. Pour the skillet contents into the crock pot over

the pork chops.4. Cover the crock pot and cook on high for 3 to 4 hours or on low for 6 to 8 hours, until the pork chops are tender. Skim off any excess fat from the top of the sauce before serving.5. Serve the pork chops directly from the slow cooker, keeping it set on warm for convenience.

Buffet Beef

Prep time: 10 minutes | Cook time: 4 to 8 hours | Serves 8 to 10

- 1 (12-ounce / 340-g) can beer
- 1 envelope dry brown gravy mix
- ⅓ cup flour
- 1 (2½- to 3-pound / 1.1- to 1.4-kg) round steak, cut into cubes

1. In the crock pot, mix the beer and gravy mix thoroughly until well combined.2. In a resealable plastic bag, add the flour and steak cubes, shaking the bag until the steak is evenly coated with the flour.3. Pour the entire contents of the bag into the crock pot and gently stir to ensure the meat is well coated with the liquid mixture.4. Cover the crock pot and cook on low for 6 to 8 hours, or on high for 4 hours, until the steak is tender and flavorful. Serve hot.

Savory Beef and Vegetable Casserole

Prep time: 20 minutes | Cook time: 4 to 5 hours | Serves 8

- 1 pound (454 g) extra-lean ground beef or turkey
- 1 medium onion, chopped
- ½ cup chopped celery
- 4 cups chopped cabbage
- 2½ cups canned stewed tomatoes, slightly mashed
- 1 tablespoon flour
- 1 teaspoon salt
- 1 tablespoon sugar
- ¼ to ½ teaspoon black pepper, according to your taste preference

1. Sauté meat, onion, and celery in nonstick skillet until meat is browned. 2. Pour into crock pot. 3. Top with layers of cabbage, tomatoes, flour, salt, sugar, and pepper. 4. Cover. Cook on high 4 to 5 hours.

Spicy Taco Beef Stew

Prep time: 15 minutes | Cook time: 7 to 8 hours | Serves 6 to 8

- 4 carrots, cubed
- 4 potatoes, peeled and cubed
- 1 onion, quartered
- 1½ pounds (680 g) beef stewing meat, cubed
- 1 (8-ounce / 227-g) can
- tomato sauce
- 1 package dry taco seasoning mix
- 2 cups water, divided
- 1½ tablespoons cornstarch
- 2 teaspoons salt
- ¼ teaspoon pepper

1. Layer first four ingredients in crock pot. Add tomato sauce. 2. Combine taco seasoning with 1½ cups water. Stir cornstarch into remaining ½ cup water until smooth. Stir into rest of water with taco seasoning. Pour over ingredients in crock pot. 3. Sprinkle with salt and pepper. 4. Cover. Cook on low 7 to 8 hours. 5. Serve.

Sugar and Spice Pork Loin

Prep time: 20 minutes | Cook time: 4 to 10 hours | Serves 6 to 8

- 2 medium sweet potatoes, peeled and cut into 1-inch chunks or wedges
- 2 medium Yukon gold potatoes, peeled and cut into 1-inch chunks or wedges
- 2 medium red onions, cut into quarters
- ½ cup olive oil
- 1 teaspoon ground cumin
- 1½ teaspoons fennel seeds
- ½ teaspoon ground cinnamon
- ½ teaspoon ground ginger
- ¼ cup firmly packed light brown sugar
- 2 teaspoons salt
- 1 teaspoon freshly ground black pepper
- 1 (4-pound / 1.8-kg) pork loin roast, rolled and tied
- ½ cup chicken broth

1. Place the vegetables in the bottom of a 5- to 7-quart crock pot. Drizzle ¼ cup of olive oil over the vegetables and toss to evenly coat. In a small bowl, mix the cumin, fennel seeds, cinnamon, ginger, sugar, salt, and pepper. Sprinkle 1 tablespoon of this spice mixture over the vegetables and toss again to ensure they're well seasoned.2. Pat the remaining spice rub all over the pork, ensuring it's evenly coated. Place the seasoned meat on top of the vegetables in the crock pot, then drizzle with the remaining ¼ cup of olive oil. Pour in the chicken broth around the sides. Cover and cook on high for 4 to 5 hours, or on low for 8 to 10 hours, until the pork and vegetables are tender and the roast reaches an internal temperature of 175°F (79°C).3. Once done, transfer the pork to a cutting board, cover it with aluminum foil, and let it rest for 20 minutes. Slice the pork into ½-inch-thick pieces and arrange them in the center of a platter. Surround the meat with the cooked vegetables and serve.

Tangy Barbecued Beef Sandwiches

Prep time: 10 minutes | Cook time: 10 to 12 hours | Makes 18 to 20 sandwiches

- 1 (3½- to 4-pound / 1.6- to 1.8-kg) beef round steak, cubed
- 1 cup finely chopped onions
- ½ cup firmly packed brown sugar
- 1 tablespoon chili powder
- ½ cup ketchup
- ⅓ cup cider vinegar
- 1 (12-ounce / 340-g) can beer
- 1 (6-ounce / 170-g) can tomato paste
- Buns

1. Combine all ingredients except buns in crock pot. 2. Cover. Cook on low 10 to 12 hours. 3. Remove beef from sauce with slotted spoon. 4. Place in large bowl. Shred with 2 forks. Add 2 cups sauce from crock pot to shredded beef. Mix well. 5. Pile into buns and serve immediately.

Mushroom-Smothered Steak

Prep time: 15 minutes | Cook time: 8½ hours | Serves 2

- 1 pound (454 g) chuck eye roast, trimmed of excess fat
- 2 tablespoons all-purpose flour, divided
- ½ teaspoon dried marjoram leaves
- ½ teaspoon salt
- ⅛ teaspoon freshly ground black pepper
- 2 tablespoons extra-virgin olive oil
- 1 cup sliced cremini mushrooms
- 1 cup sliced button mushrooms
- 1 cup sliced shiitake mushrooms
- 1 onion, chopped
- 2 garlic cloves, minced
- 1½ cups beef stock
- 1 tablespoon soy sauce
- ½ cup sour cream

1. On a platter, sprinkle the beef with 1 tablespoon of flour, along with marjoram, salt, and pepper, making sure it's evenly coated.2. Heat the oil in a large skillet over medium heat. Add the beef and brown it, turning once, for about 5 minutes total.3. In the crock pot, place the cremini, button, and shiitake mushrooms, along with the onion and garlic. Place the browned steak on top of the vegetables, then pour in the stock and soy sauce.4. Cover the crock pot and cook on low for 8 hours, allowing the flavors to meld together.5. In a medium bowl, whisk the sour cream and remaining 1 tablespoon of flour with 1 cup of the liquid from the crock pot until smooth. Stir this mixture into the crock pot.6. Cover and cook on low for an additional 20 to 30 minutes, until the sauce has thickened. Serve hot.

Tiajuana Tacos

Prep time: 20 minutes | Cook time: 2 hours | Serves 6

- 3 cups cooked chopped beef
- 1 (1-pound / 454-g) can refried beans
- ½ cup chopped onions
- ½ cup chopped green peppers
- ½ cup chopped ripe olives
- 1 (8-ounce / 227-g) can tomato sauce
- 3 teaspoons chili powder
- 1 tablespoon Worcestershire sauce
- ½ teaspoon garlic powder
- ¼ teaspoon pepper
- ¼ teaspoon paprika
- ⅛ teaspoon celery salt
- ⅛ teaspoon ground nutmeg
- ¾ cup water
- 1 teaspoon salt
- 1 cup crushed corn chips
- 6 taco shells
- Shredded lettuce
- Chopped tomatoes
- Shredded Cheddar cheese

1. Add the first 15 ingredients to the crock pot and mix well to combine.2. Cover the crock pot and cook on high for 2 hours, allowing the flavors to meld together.3. Just before serving, gently fold in the corn chips to keep them crisp.4. Spoon the mixture into taco shells and top with fresh lettuce, diced tomatoes, and shredded cheese. Serve immediately.

South Indian Coconut-Pork Curry

Prep time: 15 minutes | Cook time: 4 to 6 hours | Serves 6 to 8

- 2 pounds (907 g) boneless pork shoulder, skin removed, cut into chunks
- Sea salt
- Freshly ground black pepper
- 2 tablespoons rapeseed oil
- 2 teaspoons cumin seeds
- 1 teaspoon coriander seeds
- 2 onions, finely diced
- 5 garlic cloves, minced
- 1 fresh green chile, chopped
- 1 tablespoon freshly grated
- ginger
- 1 teaspoon ground turmeric
- 2 star anise
- 2 dried red chiles
- 7 to 8 ounces (198 to 227 g) canned tomatoes
- 1 (14-ounce / 397-g) can coconut milk
- ¼ pound (113 g) green beans, trimmed
- Handful fresh coriander leaves, chopped

1. Generously season the pork with salt and plenty of black pepper.2. Set the crock pot to high or use the sauté setting if available. Add the oil and sear the pork for 1 to 2 minutes on each side to lock in the flavor.3. Grind the cumin and coriander seeds using a mortar and pestle until fine.4. Combine the ground cumin and coriander with the onions, garlic, green chile, ginger, turmeric, anise, and red chiles, stirring everything together well.5. Blend the

tomatoes in a blender until smooth, then pour them into the crock pot along with the coconut milk. Cover the crock pot and cook on low for 6 hours or on high for 4 hours.6. Thirty minutes before the end of the cooking time, add the trimmed beans to the crock pot and cook for an additional 30 minutes.7. Once the dish is fully cooked, taste and adjust the seasoning as needed, then sprinkle with fresh coriander leaves before serving.

Slow-Cooked Pork Chops with Green Beans

Prep time: 10 minutes | Cook time: 4 to 8 hours | Serves 3 to 4

- 3 to 4 boneless pork chops
- Salt and pepper to taste
- 2 cups green beans, frozen or fresh
- 2 slices bacon, cut up
- ½ cup water
- 1 tablespoon lemon juice

1. Lay the pork chops at the bottom of the crock pot and season generously with salt and pepper to taste.2. Layer the remaining ingredients on top of the pork chops in the order they are listed, ensuring an even distribution.3. Cover the crock pot and cook on low for 4 to 8 hours, or until the pork and green beans are tender but still moist and not overcooked. Serve hot.

Hearty Election Day Bean and Sausage Stew

Prep time: 30 minutes | Cook time: 2 to 4 hours | Serves 6 to 12

- 2 to 3 tablespoons olive oil
- 1 large onion, chopped
- 1 pound (454 g) sausage, cut into thin slices, or casings removed and crumbled
- 1 rib celery, sliced
- 1 tablespoon Worcestershire sauce
- 1½ teaspoons dry mustard
- ¼ cup honey
- 1 (10-ounce / 283-g) can tomatoes with green chili peppers
- 1 (1-pound / 454-g) can lima or butter beans, drained, with liquid reserved
- 1 (1-pound / 454-g) can red kidney beans, drained, with liquid reserved
- 1 (1-pound / 454-g) can garbanzo beans, drained, with liquid reserved

1. Brown onion and sausage in oil. 2. Combine ingredients in 6-quart crock pot, or divide between 2 (4-quart) cookers and stir to combine. Add reserved juice from lima, kidney, and garbanzo beans if there's enough room in the cookers. 3. Cover. Cook on low 2 to 4 hours.

Easy Stroganoff

Prep time: 5 minutes | Cook time: 6¼ to 8¼ hours | Serves 6 to 8

- 1 (10¾-ounce / 305-g) can cream of mushroom soup
- 1 (14½-ounce / 411-g) can beef broth
- 1 pound (454 g) beef

- stewing meat or round steak, cut in 1-inch pieces
- 1 cup sour cream
- 2 cups noodles, cooked

1. In the crock pot, mix together the soup and broth until well combined. Add the meat, ensuring it is fully submerged in the mixture. 2. Cover the crock pot and cook on high for 3 to 4 hours. After that, reduce the heat to low and continue cooking for another 3 to 4 hours, allowing the flavors to develop. 3. Stir in the sour cream, blending it into the mixture thoroughly. 4. Add the noodles and stir to combine them with the sauce and meat. 5. Turn the heat back to high and cook for an additional 20 minutes, or until the noodles are fully cooked. Serve hot.

Rustic Lamb Cassoulet with White Beans and Rosemary

Prep time: 30 minutes | Cook time: 6 to 12 hours | Serves 6

- 1 pound (454 g) dried white beans, soaked in water to cover overnight and drained
- ½ cup extra-virgin olive oil
- 6 meaty lamb shanks, fat trimmed
- 1½ teaspoons salt
- ½ teaspoon freshly ground black pepper
- 3 medium onions, coarsely chopped
- 4 cloves garlic, minced
- 4 medium carrots, coarsely chopped
- 4 stalks celery, coarsely chopped

- 1 tablespoon fresh rosemary leaves, finely chopped
- 1 (28- to 32-ounce / 794- to 907-g) can crushed tomatoes, with their juice
- 5 cups chicken broth
- 3 cups beef broth
- 1 bay leaf
- Topping:
- 1½ cups fresh bread crumbs
- ½ cup freshly grated Parmigiano-Reggiano cheese
- 4 cloves garlic, minced
- ½ cup finely chopped fresh Italian parsley

1. Place the beans in the insert of a 5- to 7-quart crock pot. Heat the oil in a large skillet over medium-high heat. Sprinkle the meat evenly with the salt and pepper. Add as many lamb shanks as will fit in a single layer and brown on all sides. Transfer the browned shanks to the slow-cooker insert. Brown any remaining shanks and transfer them to the slow-cooker insert. 2. Add the onions, garlic, carrots, celery, and rosemary to the same skillet and sauté until the vegetables are softened, 5 to 7 minutes. Add the tomatoes and 1 cup of the chicken broth to the skillet and heat, scraping up any browned bits from the bottom of the pan. Transfer the tomato mixture to the slow-cooker insert and stir in the remaining broths, and the bay leaf. Cover and cook on high for 6 to 8 hours or low for 10 to 12 hours, until the beans and lamb are tender. 3. Combine all the ingredients for the topping in a small bowl while the lamb is cooking. Cover and refrigerate. 4. Uncover the cooker and spoon off any fat on the surface. Taste and adjust with the seasoning. Sprinkle the topping over the cassoulet, cover, and cook on high another 30 minutes. 5. Serve the cassoulet from the cooker set on warm.

Hearty Sauerkraut Chop Suey Stew

Prep time: 15 minutes | Cook time: 8 to 10 hours | Serves 10

- 1 pound (454 g) beef stewing meat, trimmed of fat
- 1 pound (454 g) pork roast, cubed and trimmed of fat
- 2 (10¾-ounce / 305-g) cans 98% fat-free cream of mushroom soup

- 1 envelope dry onion soup mix
- 1 (27-ounce / 765-g) can sauerkraut
- 2 cups skim milk
- 1 (12-ounce / 340-g) package kluski (or extra-sturdy) noodles

1. Combine all ingredients except noodles in crock pot. 2. Cook on low 8 to 10 hours. 3. Add uncooked noodles 2 hours before serving, or cook noodles fully, drain, and stir into chop suey 15 minutes before serving.

Fiesta Chili Mix with Fritos

Prep time: 15 minutes | Cook time: 4 hours | Serves 4 to 6

- 1 pound (454 g) ground beef
- 1 (16-ounce / 454-g) can cream-style corn, drained
- ½ cup chunky picante sauce
- 1 (16-ounce / 454-g) can pinto or black beans, drained

- Half an envelope dry taco seasoning
- Corn chips
- Shredded cheese (optional)
- Chopped olives (optional)
- Sour cream (optional)
- Salsa (optional)

1. Brown ground beef in a large nonstick skillet. Drain. 2. Mix beef, corn, picante sauce, beans, and taco seasoning in crock pot. 3. Cover and cook on low 4 hours. 4. Serve over corn chips with optional garnishes of shredded cheese, chopped olives, sour cream, and salsa.

Southwest Taco Meatloaf

Prep time: 10 minutes | Cook time: 8 to 10 hours | Serves 8

- 2½ pounds (1.1 kg) ground beef
- Half of 1 (8-ounce / 227-g) jar salsa
- 1 package dry taco seasoning, divided
- 1 egg, slightly beaten
- 1 cup bread crumbs
- 1 (12-ounce / 340-g) package shredded Mexican-mix cheese
- 2 teaspoons salt
- ½ teaspoon pepper

1. Combine all ingredients, except half of taco seasoning. Mix well. Shape into loaf and place in crock pot. Sprinkle with remaining taco seasoning. 2. Cover. Cook on low 8 to 10 hours.

China Dish

Prep time: 20 minutes | Cook time: 6 to 8 hours | Serves 6

- 1½ pounds (680 g) extra-lean ground beef
- 1 (10¾-ounce / 305-g) can cream of chicken soup
- 1 (10¾-ounce / 305-g) can 98% fat-free cream of mushroom soup
- 3½ cups water
- 2 cups chopped celery
- 1 cup chopped onions
- 1 cup brown rice, uncooked
- 3 tablespoons Worcestershire sauce

1. In a nonstick skillet, brown the ground beef over medium heat until fully cooked.2. Transfer the browned beef to the crock pot and combine it with all remaining ingredients, stirring well to mix everything together.3. Cover the crock pot and cook on low for 6 to 8 hours, allowing the flavors to meld together. Serve hot.

Slow-Cooked Barbecue Beef Roast Sandwiches

Prep time: 10 minutes | Cook time: 10 to 12 hours | Makes 10 to 12 sandwiches

- 3 to 4 pounds (1.4 to 1.8 kg) beef roast (bottom round or rump is best)
- 1 cup water, divided
- ½ cup ketchup
- 1 teaspoon chili powder
- 1½ tablespoons
- Worcestershire sauce
- 2 tablespoons vinegar
- 1 teaspoon salt
- 1 tablespoon sugar
- 1 teaspoon dry mustard
- 1 medium onion, finely chopped

1. The night before serving, place roast in crock pot with ½ cup water. 2. Cover. Cook on low 10 to 12 hours. 3. Also the night

before serving, combine remaining ingredients and refrigerate 8 to 10 hours. 4. In the morning, shred roast with fork and return to cooker. Pour remaining ingredients over top. Mix together. 5. Heat on low until mealtime. 6. Serve.

German Pot Roast

Prep time: 15 minutes | Cook time: 4 to 8 hours | Serves 12

- 2 pounds (907 g) boneless, lean pork roast
- 1 teaspoon garlic salt
- ½ teaspoon black pepper
- 4 large sweet potatoes,
- peeled and diced
- 2 medium onions, sliced
- ½ teaspoon dried oregano
- 1 (14½-ounce / 411-g) can low-sodium tomatoes

1. Place the pork roast in the crock pot, ensuring it's centered.2. Season the roast by sprinkling it with garlic salt and pepper to taste.3. Add the remaining ingredients around and on top of the pork roast.4. Cover the crock pot and cook on low for 7 to 8 hours, or on high for 4 to 5 hours, until the pork is tender and fully cooked. Serve warm.

Garlic-Infused Veal Stew

Prep time: 20 minutes | Cook time: 6 to 7 hours | Serves 6

- ½ cup all-purpose flour
- 1½ teaspoons salt
- ½ teaspoon freshly ground black pepper
- 2½ pounds (1.1 kg) boneless veal shoulder or shank, cut into 1-inch pieces
- 3 tablespoons extra-virgin olive oil
- ¼ cup tomato paste
- 1 teaspoon dried thyme
- ½ cup dry white wine or vermouth
- 1 cup chicken broth
- ½ cup beef broth
- 1 bay leaf
- 40 cloves garlic, peeled

1. Mix the flour, salt, and pepper in a large zipper-top plastic bag. Add the veal, toss to coat, and shake off any excess. Heat the oil in a large skillet over high heat. Add the veal a few pieces at a time and sauté until browned on all sides. 2. Transfer the browned meat to the insert of a 5- to 7-quart crock pot. When all the veal is browned, add the tomato paste, thyme, and white wine to the skillet and scrape up any browned bits from the bottom of the pan. Add both broths and stir to combine. 3. Pour the contents of the skillet over the veal in the crock pot, add the bay leaf and garlic, and stir to distribute the ingredients. Cover and cook the veal on low for 6 to 7 hours, until it is tender. Remove the veal from the cooker with a slotted spoon. 4. Mash the garlic cloves and stir them into the sauce. Taste and adjust the seasoning. Return the veal to the cooker and serve the stew.

Italian Beef au Jus

Prep time: 10 minutes | Cook time: 8 hours | Serves 8

- 1 (3- to 5-pound / 1.4- to 2.3-kg) boneless beef roast
- 1 (10-ounce / 283-g) package dry au jus mix
- 1 package dry Italian salad dressing mix
- 1 (14½-ounce / 411-g) can beef broth
- Half a soup can water

1. Place the beef roast in the crock pot, making sure it's centered. 2. In a bowl, mix together the remaining ingredients until well combined. Pour the mixture evenly over the beef. 3. Cover the crock pot and cook on low for 8 hours, allowing the roast to become tender and flavorful. 4. Once done, carefully slice the meat and serve hot.

Port-Braised Pork Loin with Dried Plums

Prep time: 25 minutes | Cook time: 6 to 7 hours | Serves 10

- 1 (3¼-pound / 1.5-kg) boneless pork loin roast, trimmed
- 1½ teaspoons black pepper
- 1 teaspoon sea salt
- 1 teaspoon dry mustard
- 1 teaspoon dried sage
- ½ teaspoon dried thyme
- 1 tablespoon olive oil
- 2 large yellow onions, sliced
- 1 cup finely chopped leek, white and light green parts, rinsed
- 1 large carrot, finely chopped
- ½ cup port or other sweet red wine
- ⅔ cup chicken stock
- 1 cup pitted dried plums (about 20)
- 2 bay leaves
- 2 tablespoons cornstarch
- 2 tablespoons water

1. Cut the pork roast in half crosswise. 2. Combine the pepper, salt, dry mustard, sage, and thyme in a small bowl. Rub the seasoning mixture over the surface of the roast halves. 3. Heat a Dutch oven over medium-high heat. Add the olive oil to pan and swirl to coat. Add the pork and brown on all sides, about 4 minutes. Place the pork in the crock pot. 4. Add the onions, leek, and carrot to the Dutch oven, and sauté for 5 minutes or until vegetables are golden. 5. Stir in the wine and stock, and cook for about 1 minute, scraping the bottom of the pan with a wooden spoon to loosen up the flavorful browned bits. 6. Pour the wine-vegetable mixture over the pork in crock pot. Add the plums and bay leaves. 7. Cover and cook on high for 1 hour. Reduce the heat to low, and cook for 5 to 6 hours, or until the pork is tender. 8. Remove the pork from the crock pot, set aside on a platter, and keep warm. Increase the heat to high. 9. Combine the cornstarch and 2 tablespoons water in a small bowl. Whisk to combine, and then whisk into the cooking liquid in the crock pot. 10. Cook, uncovered, for 15 minutes or until the sauce is thick, stirring frequently. 11. Discard the bay leaves. Slice the pork, and serve hot with the sauce.

Chili con Carne

Prep time: 15 minutes | Cook time: 5 to 6 hours | Serves 8

- 1 pound (454 g) ground beef
- 1 cup chopped onions
- ¾ cup chopped green peppers
- 1 garlic clove, minced
- 1 (14½-ounce / 411-g) can tomatoes, cut up
- 1 (16-ounce / 454-g) can kidney beans, drained
- 1 (8-ounce / 227-g) can tomato sauce
- 2 teaspoons chili powder
- ½ teaspoon dried basil

1. In a saucepan, brown the beef, onion, green pepper, and garlic over medium heat, stirring occasionally. Once browned, drain any excess fat. 2. Transfer the browned mixture to the crock pot and combine it with all the remaining ingredients, stirring well. 3. Cover the crock pot and cook on low for 5 to 6 hours, allowing the flavors to meld together. 4. Once done, serve hot and enjoy.

Mediterranean-Style Slow-Cooked Spareribs

Prep time: 15 minutes | Cook time: 8 to 10 hours | Serves 6

- 3 pounds (1.4 kg) country-style spareribs
- 1½ teaspoons salt
- 2 tablespoons extra-virgin olive oil
- 3 medium onions, finely chopped
- ⅛ teaspoon red pepper
- flakes
- 3 cloves garlic, minced
- 1 teaspoon dried oregano
- ½ cup red wine, such as Chianti or Barolo
- 1 (28- to 32-ounce / 794- to 907-g) can crushed tomatoes, with their juice

1. Sprinkle the ribs with the salt and arrange in the insert of a 5- to 7-quart crock pot. Heat the oil in a large skillet over medium-high heat. Add the onions, red pepper flakes, garlic, and oregano and sauté until the onions are softened, about 5 minutes. 2. Add the wine to the skillet and stir up any browned bits from the bottom of the pan. Transfer the contents of the skillet to the slow-cooker insert and stir in the tomatoes. Cover and cook on low for 8 to 10 hours, until the meat is tender. Skim off any fat from the surface of the sauce. 3. Serve the ribs from the cooker set on warm.

Soy-Ginger Pork Chops with Green Beans

Prep time: 15 minutes | Cook time: 8 hours | Serves 2

- 1 teaspoon extra-virgin olive oil
- 2 bone-in pork chops, about 8 ounces (227 g) each
- Freshly ground black pepper
- 3 cups whole green beans, stems removed
- 2 teaspoons minced fresh ginger
- 1 teaspoon minced garlic
- ¼ cup low-sodium soy sauce
- ½ cup low-sodium chicken or vegetable broth

1. Lightly grease the inside of the crock pot with olive oil to prevent sticking.2. Lay the pork chops at the bottom of the crock pot and season them with a few grinds of black pepper. Spread the green beans over the pork chops.3. In a small bowl, whisk together the ginger, garlic, soy sauce, and broth until well combined. Pour this mixture evenly over the green beans and pork.4. Cover the crock pot and cook on low for 8 hours, or until the pork is fully cooked and the green beans are tender. Serve hot.

Barbecued Brisket

Prep time: 20 minutes | Cook time: 4 to 10 hours | Serves 6 to 8

- 4 tablespoons olive oil
- 3 cloves garlic, minced
- 1½ teaspoons salt
- 1 teaspoon freshly ground black pepper
- 1 (4- to 5-pound / 1.8- to 2.3-kg) flat cut brisket, fat trimmed
- 4 large onions, thinly sliced
- 1½ cups ketchup
- 2 cups tomato purée
- 1 teaspoon Tabasco sauce
- ½ cup firmly packed light brown sugar
- ¼ cup molasses
- ¼ cup Dijon mustard

1. In a small bowl, mix together 2 tablespoons of the oil, garlic, salt, and pepper. Rub this mixture thoroughly over the entire brisket.2. Heat the remaining 2 tablespoons of oil in a large skillet over high heat. Sear the brisket on all sides until browned. Transfer the browned brisket to the insert of a 5- to 7-quart crock pot. In the same skillet, reduce the heat to medium-high and sauté the onions for 5 to 7 minutes until softened.3. Add the remaining ingredients to the skillet, stirring to combine. Pour the contents of the skillet over the brisket in the crock pot, ensuring the liquid and vegetables are evenly distributed. Cover and cook on high for 4 to 5 hours or on low for 8 to 10 hours until the brisket is tender.4. Remove the brisket from the crock pot, cover it with aluminum foil, and let it rest for 15 minutes. Meanwhile, skim any fat from the sauce in the crock pot and transfer the sauce to a saucepan. Boil the sauce for about 10 minutes to reduce and concentrate the flavor.5. Taste the

sauce and adjust the seasoning if necessary. Slice the brisket at an angle across the grain and place the slices back into the crock pot.6. Pour the reduced sauce over the brisket slices and leave the crock pot set on low until ready to serve, for up to 4 hours.

Slow-Cooked Pork Chops in Mushroom Wine Sauce

Prep time: 10 minutes | Cook time: 4½ to 10 hours | Serves 4 to 6

- 4 to 6 boneless thin or thick pork chops
- 1 (10¾-ounce / 305-g) can cream of mushroom soup
- ¾ cup white wine
- 1 (4-ounce / 113-g) can sliced mushrooms
- 2 tablespoons quick cooking tapioca
- 2 teaspoons Worcestershire sauce
- 1 teaspoon beef bouillon granules, or 1 beef bouillon cube
- ¼ teaspoon minced garlic
- ¾ teaspoon dried thyme (optional)

1. Place pork chops in crock pot. 2. Combine remaining ingredients and pour over pork chops. 3. Cook on low 8 to 10 hours, or on high 4½ to 5 hours. 4. Serve.

Orange-Cranberry Glazed Pork Roast

Prep time: 15 minutes | Cook time: 7 to 8 hours | Serves 6

- 3 tablespoons extra-virgin olive oil, divided
- 2 tablespoons butter
- 2 pounds (907 g) pork shoulder roast
- 1 teaspoon ground cinnamon
- ¼ teaspoon allspice
- ¼ teaspoon salt
- ⅛ teaspoon freshly ground black pepper
- ½ cup cranberries
- ½ cup chicken broth
- ½ cup granulated erythritol
- 2 tablespoons Dijon mustard
- Juice and zest of ½ orange
- 1 scallion, white and green parts, chopped, for garnish

1. Lightly grease the insert of the crock pot with 1 tablespoon of the olive oil. 2. In a large skillet over medium-high heat, heat the remaining 2 tablespoons of the olive oil and the butter. 3. Lightly season the pork with cinnamon, allspice, salt, and pepper. Add the pork to the skillet and brown on all sides for about 10 minutes. Transfer to the insert. 4. In a small bowl, stir together the cranberries, broth, erythritol, mustard, and orange juice and zest, and add the mixture to the pork. 5. Cover and cook on low for 7 to 8 hours. 6. Serve topped with the scallion.

Tangy Barbecue Meatballs

Prep time: 30 minutes | Cook time: 5 hours | Serves 10

Meatballs:

- ¾ pound (340 g) ground beef
- ¾ cup bread crumbs
- 1½ tablespoons minced onion
- ½ teaspoon horseradish

- 3 drops Tabasco sauce
- 2 eggs, beaten
- ¾ teaspoon salt
- ½ teaspoon pepper
- Butter

Sauce:

- ¾ cup ketchup
- ½ cup water
- ¼ cup cider vinegar
- 2 tablespoons brown sugar
- 1 tablespoon minced onion

- 2 teaspoons horseradish
- 1 teaspoon salt
- 1 teaspoon dry mustard
- 3 drops Tabasco
- Dash pepper

1. Combine all meatball ingredients except butter. 2. Shape into ¾-inch balls. Brown in butter in skillet. Place in crock pot. Combine all sauce ingredients. Pour over meatballs. 3. Cover. Cook on low 5 hours.

Kashmiri Lamb Stew

Prep time: minutes | Cook time: 4¼ to 6¼ hours | Serves 6 to 8

- 2 tablespoons mustard oil
- Large pinch asafetida
- 1 teaspoon cumin seeds
- 2¾-inch piece cassia bark
- 3 cloves
- 2 dried Kashmiri chiles
- 2 black cardamom pods
- 2 green cardamom pods
- 1 teaspoon salt
- 1¾ pounds (794 g) boneless leg of lamb, cut into large

- chunks
- 1 teaspoon red Kashmiri chili powder
- 1 teaspoon hot chili powder (optional)
- 1 teaspoon ground ginger
- 1 teaspoon ground fennel seeds
- About ¼ cup hot water
- 3 heaped tablespoons Greek yogurt
- 1 teaspoon garam masala

1. Set the crock pot to high or use the sauté function. Add the mustard oil and heat it until it reaches the smoking point, then turn off the cooker and allow the oil to cool down slightly.2. Reheat the crock pot on high and add the asafetida, followed by cumin seeds, cassia bark, cloves, whole chiles, black and green cardamom pods, and salt. Stir the spices until they become aromatic.3. Add the meat to the crock pot and stir, allowing it to sear for a few minutes until browned.4. Sprinkle in the chili powders and continue cooking the meat for a few minutes. Then, add the ginger and fennel seeds, stirring well to combine.5. Cover the crock pot and cook on low

for 6 hours or on high for 4 hours, checking halfway through. If needed, add some hot water to prevent drying out.6. Once the meat is tender, gradually stir in the yogurt, 1 tablespoon at a time, ensuring it blends smoothly into the sauce. Let it cook for an additional 15 minutes.7. Finish by adding the garam masala, check the seasoning, and adjust as necessary before serving.

Cheeseburger Casserole

Prep time: 20 minutes | Cook time: 3 hours | Serves 6

- 1 pound (454 g) ground beef
- 1 small onion, chopped
- 1 teaspoon salt
- Dash of pepper
- ½ cup bread crumbs

- 1 egg
- Tomato juice to moisten
- 4½ cups mashed potatoes
- 9 slices American cheese

1. In a bowl, mix together the beef, onions, salt, pepper, bread crumbs, egg, and tomato juice until well combined. Place one-third of this mixture into the bottom of the crock pot.2. Spread one-third of the mashed potatoes over the beef mixture, then layer with 3 slices of cheese. Repeat the layers two more times, ensuring even distribution of the ingredients.3. Cover the crock pot and cook on low for 3 hours until the dish is cooked through and the cheese is melted. Serve warm.

My Norwegian Meatballs

Prep time: 5 minutes | Cook time: 45 minutes | Serves 10 to 12

- 1 (2- to 2½-pound / 907-g to 1.1-kg) package frozen meatballs
- 2 or 3 (10¾-ounce / 305-g) cans cream of mushroom soup

- 1 (12-ounce / 340-g) can evaporated milk
- 1½ cups sour cream
- 1 cup beef broth
- 1 teaspoon dill weed (optional)

1. Arrange the frozen meatballs in a long, microwave-safe dish and microwave on high for 4 minutes to begin thawing.2. While the meatballs are in the microwave, mix together all the remaining ingredients in a large bowl until well combined.3. Transfer the partially thawed meatballs into the crock pot, then pour the prepared soup mixture over the top, ensuring the meatballs are well covered.4. Cover the crock pot and cook on high for 45 minutes, ensuring the sauce doesn't come to a boil.5. After 45 minutes, turn the crock pot to low and keep the meatballs warm until ready to serve.

Sweet and Spicy Hawaiian Sausages

Prep time: 15 minutes | Cook time: 4 to 5 hours | Serves 6 to 8

- 3 pounds (1.4 kg) link pork sausages
- 2 cups pineapple juice
- 3 tablespoons cornstarch
- 1 teaspoon curry powder
- 1 ripe large pineapple, peeled and cored, and cut into 1-inch chunks (about 4 cups)

1. Sauté the sausages in a large skillet until browned on all sides. Transfer the sausages to the insert of a 5- to 7-quart crock pot. 2. Mix the pineapple juice, cornstarch, and curry powder in a mixing bowl, and pour into the slow-cooker insert. Add the pineapple, cover, and cook on low for 4 to 5 hours, until the sausages are cooked through and the sauce is thickened. 3. Serve from the cooker set on warm.

Light and Creamy Beef Casserole

Prep time: 5 minutes | Cook time: 6 to 8 hours | Serves 5

- 1 pound (454 g) extra-lean ground beef
- 1 package dry onion soup mix
- 1 (10¾-ounce / 305-g)
- can 98% fat-free cream of celery soup
- 1 (10¾-ounce / 305-g) can 98% fat-free cream of mushroom soup

1. Spray crock pot with fat-free cooking spray. 2. Combine all ingredients in crock pot. 3. Cook on low for 6 to 8 hours. 4. Serve.

Barbecued Pot Roast

Prep time: 5 minutes | Cook time: 5 to 6 hours | Serves 10

- 1 (5-pound / 2.3-kg) roast
- 1 (16-ounce / 454-g) bottle honey barbecue sauce
- 1 small onion, chopped
- 1 clove garlic, minced
- Black pepper (optional)
- Montreal seasoning (optional)

1. Place the roast in the crock pot, ensuring it's centered.2. Pour the barbecue sauce evenly over the top of the roast.3. Sprinkle the chopped onion on top of the roast and place the garlic cloves beside it.4. If desired, sprinkle the roast with pepper and/or Montreal seasoning for added flavor.5. Cover the crock pot and cook on low for 5 to 6 hours, until the roast is tender.6. Once done, remove the roast from the crock pot and let it rest for 10 minutes before slicing. Serve the sliced roast with the cooking juices.

Lamb Shanks and Potatoes

Prep time: 10 minutes | Cook time: 5 to 8 hours | Serves 6

- 1 (15-ounce / 425-g) can crushed tomatoes in purée
- 3 tablespoons tomato paste
- 2 tablespoons apricot jam
- 6 cloves garlic, thinly sliced
- 3 strips orange zest
- ¾ teaspoon crushed dried rosemary
- ½ teaspoon ground ginger
- ½ teaspoon ground
- cinnamon
- Coarse sea salt
- Black pepper
- 3½ pounds (1.6 kg) lamb shanks, trimmed of excess fat and cut into 1½-inch slices
- 1¼ pounds (567 g) small new potatoes, halved (or quartered, if large)

1. In the crock pot, stir together the tomatoes and purée, tomato paste, jam, garlic, orange zest, rosemary, ginger, and cinnamon until well combined. Season with salt and pepper to taste.2. Add the lamb and potatoes to the crock pot, and spoon the tomato mixture over the lamb to ensure it's well coated.3. Cover and cook on low for 8 hours or on high for 5 hours, until the lamb and potatoes are tender. Taste and adjust seasoning with more salt and pepper if desired.4. Serve the dish hot and enjoy.

Cheesy Beef and Macaroni Delight

Prep time: 20 minutes | Cook time: 1½ hours | Serves 5

- 1 pound (454 g) ground beef
- 1 small onion, chopped
- 3 cups dry macaroni
- 1 cup shredded Cheddar cheese
- 4 cups spaghetti sauce, your favorite packaged or homemade
- ½ cup water
- Nonstick cooking spray

1. Brown beef with chopped onion in a nonstick skillet. Drain. 2. Spray interior of crock pot with nonstick cooking spray. Place all ingredients into crock pot and fold together gently. 3. Cover and cook on high for 1½ hours, or until macaroni is tender but not mushy.

Salisbury Steak

- 3 tablespoons extra-virgin olive oil, divided
- 1½ pounds (680 g) ground beef
- ½ cup almond flour
- ¼ cup heavy (whipping) cream
- 1 scallion, white and green parts, chopped
- 1 egg
- 1 teaspoon minced garlic
- 2 cups sliced mushrooms

- ½ sweet onion, chopped
- 1½ cups beef broth
- 1 tablespoon Dijon mustard
- ¾ cup heavy (whipping) cream
- Salt, for seasoning
- Freshly ground black pepper, for seasoning
- 2 tablespoons chopped fresh parsley, for garnish

1. Lightly grease the crock pot insert with 1 tablespoon of olive oil. 2. In a medium bowl, combine the beef, almond flour, heavy cream, scallion, egg, and garlic. Mix well and form the mixture into 6 patties, about 1 inch thick. 3. Heat the remaining 2 tablespoons of olive oil in a large skillet over medium-high heat. Pan sear the patties for about 5 minutes on each side, then transfer them to the crock pot insert. 4. In the same skillet, sauté the mushrooms and onion for 3 minutes until slightly softened. 5. Whisk the broth and mustard into the skillet, scraping up any browned bits, then pour the sauce into the crock pot over the patties. 6. Cover and cook on low for 6 hours, allowing the flavors to meld. 7. When done, remove the patties from the crock pot and set them aside on a plate. Whisk the cream into the sauce in the crock pot to create a creamy texture. 8. Season the sauce with salt and pepper to taste. 9. Serve the patties topped with the creamy sauce, and garnish with fresh parsley for a finishing touch.

Braised Lamb Shanks with Olives and Potatoes

- 1¼ pounds (567 g) small potatoes, halved
- 4 large shallots, cut into ½-inch wedges
- 3 cloves garlic, minced
- 1 tablespoon lemon zest
- 3 sprigs fresh rosemary
- Coarse sea salt
- Black pepper

- 4 tablespoons all-purpose flour
- ¾ cup chicken stock
- 3½ pounds (1.6 kg) lamb shanks, cut crosswise into 1½-inch pieces and fat trimmed
- 2 tablespoons extra-virgin olive oil
- ½ cup dry white wine
- 1 cup pitted green olives, halved
- 2 tablespoons lemon juice

1. Combine the potatoes, shallots, garlic, lemon zest, and rosemary sprigs in the crock pot. Season with salt and pepper. 2. In a small bowl, whisk together 1 tablespoon of the flour and the stock. Add to the crock pot. 3. Place the remaining 3 tablespoons flour on a plate. Season the lamb with salt and pepper; then coat in the flour, shaking off any excess. 4. In a large skillet over medium-high, heat the olive oil. In batches, cook the lamb until browned on all sides, about 10 minutes. Transfer to the crock pot. 5. Add the wine to the skillet and cook, stirring with a wooden spoon and scraping up the flavorful browned bits from the bottom of the pan, until reduced by half, about 2 minutes. Then add to the crock pot. 6. Cover and cook until the lamb is tender, on high for about 3½ hours, or on low for 7 hours. 7. Stir in olive halves, then cover, and cook 20 additional minutes. 8. To serve, transfer the lamb and vegetables to warm plates. 9. Skim the fat from the cooking liquid, then stir in the lemon juice, and season the sauce with salt and pepper. 10. Serve the sauce with the lamb and vegetables.

Chapter **5**

Fish and Seafood

Chapter 5 Fish and Seafood

Bayou Shrimp and Okra Gumbo

Prep time: 35 minutes | Cook time: 5 hours | Serves 6

- ½ pound (227 g) bacon strips, chopped
- 3 celery ribs, chopped
- 1 medium onion, chopped
- 1 medium green pepper, chopped
- 2 garlic cloves, minced
- 2 (8-ounce / 227-g) bottles clam juice
- 1 (14½-ounce / 411-g) can diced tomatoes, undrained
- 2 tablespoons Worcestershire sauce
- 1 teaspoon kosher salt
- 1 teaspoon dried marjoram
- 2 pounds (907 g) uncooked large shrimp, peeled and deveined
- 2½ cups frozen sliced okra, thawed
- Hot cooked rice

1. In a large skillet, cook bacon over medium heat until crisp. Remove to paper towels with a slotted spoon; drain, reserving 2 tablespoons drippings. Saute the celery, onion, green pepper and garlic in drippings until tender. 2. Transfer to a 4-quart crock pot. Stir in the bacon, clam juice, tomatoes, Worcestershire sauce, salt and marjoram. Cover and cook on low for 4 hours. 3. Stir in shrimp and okra. Cover and cook 1 hour longer or until shrimp turn pink and okra is heated through. Serve with rice.

Shrimp with Marinara Sauce

Prep time: 15 minutes | Cook time: 6 to 7 hours | Serves 4

- 1 (15-ounce / 425-g) can diced tomatoes, with the juice
- 1 (6-ounce / 170-g) can tomato paste
- 1 clove garlic, minced
- 2 tablespoons minced fresh flat-leaf parsley
- ½ teaspoon dried basil
- 1 teaspoon dried oregano
- 1 teaspoon garlic powder
- 1½ teaspoons sea salt
- ¼ teaspoon black pepper
- 1 pound (454 g) cooked shrimp, peeled and deveined
- 2 cups hot cooked spaghetti or linguine, for serving
- ½ cup grated Parmesan cheese, for serving

1. In the crock pot, combine the tomatoes, tomato paste, and minced garlic. Sprinkle the mixture with parsley, basil, oregano, garlic powder, salt, and pepper. Stir to evenly distribute the seasonings.2.

Cover the crock pot and cook on low for 6 to 7 hours, allowing the flavors to meld.3. Turn the heat to high, stir in the cooked shrimp, and cover again. Cook on high for an additional 15 minutes until the shrimp is heated through.4. Serve the sauce hot over cooked pasta and top with freshly grated Parmesan cheese. Enjoy!

Beantown Butter Scallops

Prep time: 10 minutes | Cook time: 4½ hours | Serves 6

- 1 cup (2 sticks) unsalted butter
- 2 tablespoons olive oil
- 2 cloves garlic, minced
- 2 teaspoons sweet paprika
- ¼ cup dry sherry
- 2 pounds (907 g) dry-pack sea scallops
- ½ cup finely chopped fresh Italian parsley

1. Put the butter, oil, garlic, paprika, and sherry in the insert of a 5- to 7-quart slower cooker. 2. Cover and cook on low for 4 hours. Turn the cooker to high and add the scallops, tossing them in the butter sauce. Cover and cook on high for 30 to 40 minutes, until the scallops are opaque. 3. Transfer the scallops and sauce from the crock pot to a serving platter. Sprinkle with the parsley and serve.

Salmon with Lime Juice

Prep time: 10 minutes | Cook time: 2 hours | Serves 2

- 2 (6-ounce / 170-g) salmon fillets
- 1 tablespoon olive oil
- ½ tablespoon lime juice
- 2 cloves garlic, minced
- 1 teaspoon finely chopped fresh parsley
- ¼ teaspoon black pepper

1. Lay a sheet of foil on the countertop and place the salmon fillets in the center.2. In a small bowl, mix together the olive oil, lime juice, garlic, parsley, and black pepper. Brush this mixture evenly over the salmon fillets. Fold the foil over the salmon and crimp the edges tightly to create a sealed packet.3. Place the foil packet into the crock pot. Cover and cook on high for 2 hours.4. The salmon is done when it flakes easily with a fork. Serve the fillets hot, directly from the packet.

Spicy Barbecued Scallops and Shrimp

Prep time: 20 minutes | Cook time: 1 hour | Serves 2

- ½ teaspoon paprika
- ½ teaspoon garlic powder
- ¼ teaspoon onion powder
- ¼ teaspoon cayenne pepper
- ¼ teaspoon dried oregano
- ¼ teaspoon dried thyme
- ½ teaspoon sea salt
- ½ teaspoon black pepper
- 2 cloves garlic, minced
- ½ cup olive oil
- ¼ cup Worcestershire sauce
- 1 tablespoon hot pepper sauce (like Tabasco)
- Juice of 1 lemon
- 1 pound (454 g) scallops
- 1 pound (454 g) large shrimp, unpeeled
- 1 green onion, finely chopped

1. In a small bowl, mix together the paprika, garlic powder, onion powder, cayenne pepper, oregano, thyme, ½ teaspoon of salt, and ¼ teaspoon of black pepper.2. Add the paprika blend, minced garlic, olive oil, Worcestershire sauce, hot pepper sauce, and lemon juice to the crock pot. Season with additional salt and pepper to taste.3. Cover the crock pot and cook on high for 30 minutes, allowing the sauce to heat up and the flavors to combine.4. Rinse and drain the scallops and shrimp thoroughly.5. Once the sauce is hot, spoon half of it from the crock pot into a glass measuring cup and set aside.6. Place the scallops and shrimp into the crock pot with the remaining sauce, drizzle the reserved sauce from the measuring cup over the seafood, and stir gently to coat.7. Cover and cook on high for another 30 minutes, until the scallops and shrimp are opaque and cooked through.8. Turn the crock pot to the warm setting for serving. Sprinkle with chopped green onion and serve immediately.

Low Country Seafood Boil

Prep time: 15 minutes | Cook time: 6 hours | Serves 8

- 8 medium red potatoes
- 2 large, sweet onions, such as Vidalia, quartered
- 2 pounds (907 g) smoked sausage, cut into 3-inch pieces
- 1 (3-ounce / 85-g) package seafood boil seasoning
- 1 (12-ounce / 340-g) bottle pale ale beer
- 10 cups water
- 4 ears of corn, halved
- 2 pounds (907 g) medium raw shrimp, shelled and deveined
- Cocktail sauce, for serving
- Hot sauce, for serving
- ½ cup melted butter, for serving
- 1 large lemon, cut into wedges, for garnish

1. In the crock pot, combine the potatoes, onions, smoked sausage, seafood boil seasoning, beer, and water. Stir everything together until well mixed. Cover the crock pot and cook on low for 6 hours, or until the potatoes are tender when pierced with a fork.2. About 45 minutes before serving, add the corn to the crock pot. Cover again and cook for an additional 25 minutes. Then, add the shrimp, cover, and continue cooking until the shrimp turn pink and are no longer translucent.3. Once done, carefully drain the crock pot and discard the cooking liquid. Serve the seafood with cocktail sauce, hot sauce, melted butter, and lemon wedges for dipping and garnish.

Lemon Garlic Butter Halibut

Prep time: 15 minutes | Cook time: 5 hours | Serves 6

- 1 cup (2 sticks) unsalted butter
- ½ cup olive oil
- 6 cloves garlic, sliced
- 1 teaspoon sweet paprika
- ½ cup lemon juice
- Grated zest of 1 lemon
- ¼ cup finely chopped fresh chives
- 2 to 3 pounds (907 g to 1.4 kg) halibut fillets
- ½ cup finely chopped fresh Italian parsley

1. Combine the butter, oil, garlic, paprika, lemon juice, zest, and chives in the insert of a 5- to 7-quart crock pot and stir to combine. Cover and cook on low for 4 hours. 2. Add the halibut to the pot, spooning the sauce over the halibut. Cover and cook for an additional 40 minutes, until the halibut is cooked through and opaque. 3. Sprinkle the parsley evenly over the fish, and serve immediately.

Garlic-Butter Crab Claws

Prep time: 10 minutes | Cook time: 5½ hours | Serves 6 to 8

- 1 cup (2 sticks) unsalted butter
- ½ cup olive oil
- 10 cloves garlic, sliced
- 2 tablespoons Old Bay seasoning
- 2 cups dry white wine or vermouth
- 1 lemon, thinly sliced
- 3 to 4 pounds (1.4 to 1.8 kg) cooked crab legs and claws, cracked

1. Put the butter, oil, garlic, seasoning, wine, and lemon in the insert of a 5- to 7-quart crock pot. 2. Cover and cook on low for 4 hours. Add the crab, spoon the sauce over the crab, and cook for an additional 1½ hours, turning the crab in the sauce during cooking. 3. Serve the crab from the cooker set on warm.

Spicy Tomato Basil Mussels

Prep time: 15 minutes | Cook time: 7 hours | Serves 4

- 3 tablespoons olive oil
- 4 cloves garlic, minced
- 3 shallot cloves, minced
- 8 ounces (227 g) mushrooms, diced
- 1 (28-ounce / 794-g) can diced tomatoes, with the juice
- ¾ cup white wine
- 2 tablespoons dried oregano
- ½ tablespoon dried basil
- ½ teaspoon black pepper
- 1 teaspoon paprika
- ¼ teaspoon red pepper flakes
- 3 pounds (1.4 kg) mussels

1. In a large sauté pan, heat the olive oil over medium-high heat. Add the garlic, shallots, and mushrooms, cooking for 2 to 3 minutes until the garlic turns slightly brown and fragrant. Transfer the entire mixture from the pan into the crock pot.2. Add the tomatoes and white wine to the crock pot, then sprinkle with oregano, basil, black pepper, paprika, and red pepper flakes. Stir everything together.3. Cover the crock pot and cook on low for 4 to 5 hours, or on high for 2 to 3 hours, until the mushrooms are fork-tender.4. While the mushroom mixture is cooking, clean and debeard the mussels, discarding any that are open or damaged.5. Once the mushroom mixture is ready, turn the crock pot to high. Add the cleaned mussels and secure the lid tightly. Cook for an additional 30 minutes, or until the mussels open up.6. To serve, ladle the mussels into bowls with plenty of broth, discarding any mussels that didn't open. Serve hot, along with crusty bread to soak up the flavorful sauce.

Mediterranean Cod Gratin with Three Cheeses

Prep time: 20 minutes | Cook time: 1 hour | Serves 6

- 6 tablespoons olive oil
- 3 tablespoons all-purpose flour
- 1½ teaspoons sea salt
- ½ tablespoon dry mustard
- 1 teaspoon rosemary
- ¼ tablespoon ground nutmeg
- 1¼ cups milk
- 2 teaspoons lemon juice
- ⅓ cup grated Parmesan cheese
- ⅓ cup grated Asiago cheese
- ⅓ cup grated Romano cheese
- 3 pounds (1.4 kg) Pacific cod fillets

Make the Orange Layer: 1. Heat the olive oil in a small saucepan over medium heat. Stir in the flour, salt, mustard, rosemary, and nutmeg. 2. Gradually add the milk, stirring constantly until thickened. 3. Add the lemon juice, and the Parmesan, Asiago, and Romano cheeses to the saucepan. Stir until the cheeses are melted.

4. Place the fish into the crock pot, and spoon the cheese sauce over the fish. Cover and cook on high for 1 to 1½ hours or until the fish flakes. Serve hot.

Pacifica Sweet-Hot Salmon

Prep time: 10 minutes | Cook time: 1½ hours | Serves 6

- 3 pounds (1.4 kg) salmon fillets
- ½ cup Colman's English mustard
- ¼ cup honey
- 2 tablespoons finely chopped fresh dill

1. Place the salmon fillets in the insert of a 5- to 7-quart crock pot, arranging them evenly. In a small bowl, mix together the mustard, honey, and dill until well combined.2. Pour the mustard-honey mixture over the salmon, making sure to spread it evenly across the fillets.3. Cover the crock pot and cook on high for 1½ hours, or until the salmon is fully cooked and flakes easily with a fork.4. Serve the salmon directly from the crock pot, topped with some of the remaining sauce for added flavor. Enjoy!

Potato-Crusted Sea Bass

Prep time: 15 minutes | Cook time: 1½ hours | Serves 6

- 1 cup (2 sticks) unsalted butter, melted and cooled
- ½ cup fresh lemon juice
- Grated zest of 1 lemon
- 2 cloves garlic, minced
- 8 tablespoons olive oil
- 2 tablespoons Old Bay
- seasoning
- 2 to 3 pounds (907 g to 1.4 kg) sea bass fillets, cut to fit the slow-cooker insert
- 6 medium Yukon gold potatoes, cut into ¼-inch-thick slices

1. In a small bowl, stir together the butter, lemon juice, lemon zest, garlic, and 2 tablespoons of olive oil. In a separate large mixing bowl, combine the remaining 6 tablespoons of olive oil with the seasoning.2. Brush the sea bass with a portion of the butter sauce and set it aside. Toss the potatoes in the seasoned oil until well coated. Pour half of the butter sauce into the bottom of a 5- to 7-quart crock pot insert.3. Layer half of the potatoes at the bottom of the crock pot. Place the sea bass on top of the potatoes and pour half of the remaining butter sauce over the fish. Layer the remaining potatoes on top of the sea bass and drizzle with the rest of the butter sauce.4. Cover the crock pot and cook on high for 1½ hours, until the potatoes start to turn golden and the sea bass is cooked through and opaque in the center. Remove the lid and continue cooking for an additional 15 to 20 minutes to crisp the potatoes.5. Serve the dish immediately while hot. Enjoy!

Savory Salmon Cakes with White Wine Butter Sauce

Prep time: 15 minutes | Cook time: 5 hours | Serves 6

White Wine Butter Sauce:

- ½ cup (1 stick) unsalted butter
- 1 teaspoon Old Bay seasoning

Salmon Cakes:

- 4 cups cooked salmon, flaked
- 1 (6-ounce / 170-g) jar marinated artichoke hearts, drained and coarsely chopped
- 1 cup fresh bread crumbs

- 2 cloves garlic, sliced
- 2 ½ cups white wine or vermouth

- ½ cup freshly grated Parmigiano-Reggiano cheese
- 1 large egg, beaten
- ½ teaspoon freshly ground black pepper

1. Put all the sauce ingredients in the insert of a 5- to 7-quart crock pot and stir to combine. Cover and cook on low for 4 hours. 2. Put all the salmon cake ingredients in a large mixing bowl and stir to combine. Form the mixture into 2-inch cakes. Place the cakes in the simmering sauce and spoon the sauce over the cakes. 3. Cover and cook for an additional 1 hour, until the cakes are tender. Carefully remove the cakes to a serving platter. 4. Strain the sauce through a fine-mesh sieve into a saucepan. Bring the sauce to a boil and reduce by half. 5. Serve the sauce over the cakes, or serve on the side.

Mahi-Mahi with Tropical Salsa and Orange Lentils

Prep time: 30 minutes | Cook time: 6 hours | Serves 6

- 1¼ cups vegetable or chicken stock
- 1 cup orange juice
- ¾ cup orange lentils
- ½ cup finely diced carrot
- ¼ cup finely diced red onion
- ¼ cup finely diced celery
- 1 tablespoon honey
- 6 (4- to-5-ounce / 113- to 142-g) mahi-mahi fillets
- Sea salt
- Black pepper

- 1 teaspoon lemon juice
- Salsa:
- ¾ cup finely diced pineapple
- ¾ cup finely diced mango
- ½ cup finely diced strawberries
- ¼ cup finely diced red onion
- 2 tablespoons chopped fresh mint (or 2 teaspoons dried)
- 2 tablespoons orange juice
- 1 tablespoon lime juice
- ¼ teaspoon salt

1. Combine the stock, orange juice, lentils, carrot, onion, celery, and honey in the crock pot. 2. Cover and cook on low for 5 to 5½ hours, or until the lentils are tender. 3. Place 1 sheet of parchment paper over the lentils in the crock pot. Season mahi-mahi lightly with salt and black pepper and place it on the parchment (skin-side down, if you have not removed the skin). Replace the lid and continue to cook on low for 25 minutes or until the mahi-mahi is opaque in the center. Remove the fish by lifting out the parchment paper and putting it on a plate. 4. Stir the lemon juice into the lentils and season with salt and pepper. Make the Salsa: 5. While the fish is cooking, combine the pineapple, mango, strawberries, red onion, mint, orange juice, lime juice, and salt into a big jar. Combine and chill to give the flavors a chance to blend. 6. To serve, place about ½ cup of hot lentils on a plate and top with a mahimahi fillet and ⅓ cup of salsa.

Sea Bass Tagine

Prep time: 25 minutes | Cook time: 6 to 7½ hours | Serves 6

- 2 pounds (907 g) sea bass fillets
- ½ cup olive oil
- Grated zest of 1 lemon
- ¼ cup lemon juice
- 1 teaspoon sweet paprika
- ½ cup finely chopped fresh cilantro
- 2 cloves garlic, chopped
- 1 medium onion, finely chopped
- 1 teaspoon ground cumin

- ½ teaspoon saffron threads, crushed
- 1 (28- to 32-ounce / 794- to 907-g) can crushed tomatoes, with their juice
- 6 medium Yukon gold potatoes, quartered
- 1 teaspoon salt
- ½ teaspoon freshly ground black pepper
- ½ cup finely chopped fresh Italian parsley

1. Place the fish in a zipper-top plastic bag. 2. In a small bowl, whisk together ¼ cup of the oil, lemon zest, lemon juice, paprika, and cilantro. Pour this marinade over the fish in the bag, seal it, and refrigerate for at least 1 hour or up to 4 hours. 3. Heat the remaining ¼ cup of oil in a large skillet over medium-high heat. Add the garlic, onion, cumin, and saffron, sautéing for 5 to 7 minutes until the onion softens. 4. Stir in the tomatoes and combine well. Place the potatoes in the bottom of a 5- to 7-quart crock pot, season with salt and pepper, and toss to coat. Pour the tomato mixture over the potatoes. Cover and cook on low for 5 to 6 hours, until the potatoes are nearly tender. 5. Add the fish marinade to the crock pot, stirring to mix the potatoes and sauce. Place the marinated fish on top of the potatoes and spoon some sauce over it. Cook for an additional 1 to 1½ hours, until the sea bass is fully cooked and opaque in the center. 6. Before serving, sprinkle the sea bass with fresh parsley. Serve immediately, ensuring each plate gets some potatoes and sauce along with the fish.

Cajun Shrimp and Andouille Sausage Stew

Prep time: 15 minutes | Cook time: 3½ to 7 hours | Serves 6

- ¾ pound (340 g) andouille sausage, cut into ½-inch rounds (you may substitute Kiel-basa if you cannot find andouille sausage)
- 1 red onion, sliced into wedges
- 2 garlic cloves, minced
- 2 celery stalks, coarsely chopped
- 1 red or green bell pepper, coarsely chopped
- 2 tablespoons all-purpose flour
- 1 (28-ounce / 794-g) can diced tomatoes, with their juice
- ¼ teaspoon cayenne pepper
- Coarse sea salt
- ½ pound (227 g) large shrimp, peeled and deveined
- 2 cups fresh okra, sliced (you may substitute frozen and thawed, if necessary)

1. Put the sausage, onion, garlic, celery, and bell pepper into the crock pot. Sprinkle with the flour and toss to coat. 2. Add the tomatoes and ½ cup water. Sprinkle with the cayenne pepper and season with salt. 3. Cover and cook on high for 3½ hours or on low for 7 hours, until the vegetables are tender. 4. Add the shrimp and okra. Cover and cook until the shrimp are opaque throughout, on high for 30 minutes or on low for 1 hour. Serve hot.

Provencal Poached Salmon with Herb Cream Sauce

Prep time: 15 minutes | Cook time: 1½ to 2 hours | Serves 6

- 3 pounds (1.4 kg) salmon fillets
- ½ cup dry white wine or vermouth
- 4 cloves garlic, peeled
- 1½ teaspoons finely chopped fresh rosemary
- 2 teaspoons finely chopped fresh thyme leaves
- 2 teaspoons finely chopped fresh tarragon
- ½ cup olive oil
- 1 (28- to 32-ounce / 794- to 907-g) can plum tomatoes, drained
- ½ cup heavy cream
- Salt and freshly ground black pepper

1. Place the salmon in the insert of a 5- to 7-quart crock pot and pour in the white wine. 2. Put the garlic, rosemary, thyme, tarragon, oil, and tomatoes in a food processor and process until smooth. Spoon the mixture over the salmon in the slow-cooker insert. 3. Cover and cook on high for 1½ to 2 hours, until the fish is cooked through. 4. Transfer the salmon from the slow-cooker insert to a serving platter and remove the skin. transfer the sauce to a saucepan and bring to a boil, reducing the sauce by about ¼ cup. Add the heavy cream and stir to combine. Season with the salt and pepper. 5. Serve the salmon and top with some of the sauce.

Lemon-Dijon Salmon with Dill Barley

Prep time: 15 minutes | Cook time: 2 hours | Serves 6

- 1 medium yellow onion, diced
- 2 teaspoons garlic, minced
- 2 teaspoons olive oil
- 2 cups vegetable or chicken stock
- 1 cup quick-cooking barley
- 1 tablespoon minced fresh dill weed
- 1½ pounds (680 g) salmon fillets
- Sea salt
- Black pepper
- Lemon-Dijon Sauce:
- ⅓ cup Dijon mustard
- 3 tablespoons olive oil
- 3 tablespoons fresh lemon juice
- ⅓ cup plain Greek yogurt
- 1 clove garlic, minced

1. In a microwave-safe bowl, combine the onion, garlic, and oil. Microwave on 70 percent power for 4 to 5 minutes, stirring occasionally. Once done, transfer the mixture to the crock pot.2. Add the stock, barley, and dill weed to the crock pot and stir to combine.3. Season the salmon fillets with salt and pepper, then gently place them on top of the barley mixture in the crock pot.4. Cover and cook on low for about 2 hours, until both the salmon and barley are fully cooked.5. For the Lemon-Dijon Sauce: In a small bowl, whisk together the Dijon mustard, olive oil, lemon juice, Greek yogurt, and garlic. Set aside to let the flavors blend.6. To serve, spoon some barley onto a plate, place a salmon fillet on top, and drizzle the lemon-Dijon sauce over the salmon. Enjoy!

Spicy Seafood Laksa

Prep time: 30 minutes | Cook time: 2½ hours | Serves 6 to 8

- 2 tablespoons virgin coconut oil or extra-virgin olive oil
- 1 small onion, chopped
- 4 Thai bird chiles
- 1 (2-inch) piece fresh ginger, peeled and grated
- 1 (1-inch) piece fresh turmeric, peeled and grated
- 1 lemongrass stalk, tough outer leaves discarded, inner bulb chopped
- ¼ cup fresh cilantro
- 1 tablespoon tamarind paste
- ½ teaspoon ground cumin
- ½ teaspoon paprika
- 2 teaspoon coarse salt

- 2 cups unsweetened coconut milk
- 2 cups boiling water
- 4 kaffir lime leaves
- 2 teaspoon fish sauce
- 1 pound (454 g) medium shrimp, peeled and deveined (shells rinsed and reserved)
- 2 pounds (907 g) small mussels, scrubbed
- ¾ pound (340 g) firm fish fillet, such as halibut or cod, cut into 1-inch pieces
- 8 ounces (227 g) rice noodles
- Lime wedges, cubed firm tofu, sliced scallions, sliced Thai bird chiles, cilantro, and chili oil, for serving

1. Preheat a 7-quart crock pot. 2. Heat oil in a saucepan over medium. Add onion and cook until translucent, about 5 minutes. Add chiles, ginger, turmeric, lemongrass, cilantro, tamarind paste, cumin, paprika, and salt. Cook until fragrant, about 2 more minutes. Remove from heat and let cool. Transfer spice mixture to a food processor and puree to a thick paste. 3. Combine laksa paste, coconut milk, the boiling water, lime leaves, fish sauce, and shrimp shells in the crock pot. Cover and cook on low for 2 hours (we prefer this recipe on low). 4. Strain liquid through a medium sieve into a bowl, pressing down on solids; return broth to crock pot (discard solids). Add shrimp and mussels, and cook on low 20 minutes. Add fish and cook until shrimp is completely cooked through, fish is firm, and mussels open, about 10 minutes. 5. Meanwhile, prepare noodles according to package instructions. 6. To serve, divide noodles among bowls. Add broth and seafood, and top with tofu, scallions, chiles, and cilantro. Serve with lime wedges and chili oil.

Bouillabaisse

Prep time: 25 minutes | Cook time: 7 to 9 hours | Serves 6 to 8

- ¼ cup extra-virgin olive oil
- 3 leeks, cleaned and coarsely chopped, using the white and tender green parts
- 4 cloves garlic, sliced
- 1 bulb fennel, ends trimmed, coarsely chopped
- Grated zest of 1 orange
- 1 teaspoon dried thyme
- 1 teaspoon saffron threads, crushed
- Pinch of cayenne pepper

- 1 (28- to 32-ounce / 794- to 907-g) can crushed tomatoes, with their juice
- ½ cup white wine or dry vermouth
- 3 cups clam juice
- 1 cup chicken broth
- ½ pound (227 g) littleneck clams
- ½ pound (227 g) mussels
- 3 pounds (1.4 kg) thick-fleshed fish, cut into 1-inch chunks
- ½ cup finely chopped fresh Italian parsley

1. Heat the oil in a large skillet over medium-high heat. Add the leeks, garlic, fennel, lemon zest, thyme, saffron, and cayenne, and sauté for about 2 minutes, until the vegetables soften. Stir in the tomatoes and wine, cooking down the mixture for 10 minutes to concentrate the flavors. Transfer this mixture to the insert of a 5- to 7-quart crock pot. 2. Add the clam juice and broth to the crock pot and stir everything together. Cover and cook on low for 6 to 8 hours, allowing the flavors to develop. Remove the cover and gently place the clams and mussels into the sauce. 3. Lay the fish fillets on top of the shellfish and spoon some of the sauce over the fish. Cover and cook on high for 45 minutes, or until the fish is cooked through and opaque, and the clams and mussels have opened. 4. Discard any clams or mussels that did not open. Sprinkle the dish with fresh parsley and serve immediately. Enjoy!

Chapter **6**

Stews and Soups

Chapter 6 Stews and Soups

Taco Bean Soup

Prep time: 10 minutes | Cook time: 1½ hours | Serves 12

- ¾ pound (340 g) lean pork sausage
- 1 pound (454 g) extra-lean ground beef
- 1 envelope dry low-sodium taco seasoning
- 4 cups water
- 2 (16-ounce / 454-g) cans kidney beans, rinsed and
- drained
- 2 (14½-ounce / 411-g) cans low-sodium stewed tomatoes
- 2 (14½-ounce / 411-g) cans diced Mexican tomatoes with juice
- 1 (16-ounce / 454-g) jar chunky salsa

1. In a nonstick skillet over medium heat, cook the sausage and beef together until they are no longer pink. Once cooked, transfer the mixture to the crock pot.2. Add the taco seasoning to the crock pot and mix thoroughly to ensure the meat is well seasoned.3. Stir in the water, beans, tomatoes, and salsa, making sure everything is well combined.4. Cover the crock pot and cook on high for 1 hour, allowing the flavors to blend.5. Uncover and continue cooking for another 30 minutes, stirring occasionally to prevent sticking. Serve hot and enjoy!

Chipotle Chicken Chili

Prep time: 20 minutes | Cook time: 7 to 8 hours | Serves 6

- 3 tablespoons extra-virgin olive oil, divided
- 1 pound (454 g) ground chicken
- ½ sweet onion, chopped
- 2 teaspoons minced garlic
- 1 (28-ounce / 794-g) can diced tomatoes
- 1 cup chicken broth
- 1 cup diced pumpkin
- 1 green bell pepper, diced
- 3 tablespoons chili powder
- 1 teaspoon chipotle chili powder
- 1 cup sour cream, for garnish
- 1 cup shredded Cheddar cheese, for garnish

1. Lightly grease the crock pot insert with 1 tablespoon of olive oil to prevent sticking.2. In a large skillet over medium-high heat, heat the remaining 2 tablespoons of olive oil. Add the chicken and sauté for about 6 minutes until fully cooked.3. Add the onion and garlic to the skillet with the chicken and sauté for an additional 3 minutes until the onion softens and becomes fragrant.4. Transfer the chicken mixture to the crock pot, then stir in the tomatoes, broth, pumpkin, bell pepper, chili powder, and chipotle chili powder until well combined.5. Cover the crock pot and cook on low for 7 to 8 hours, allowing the flavors to meld and the dish to fully cook.6. Serve the dish topped with a dollop of sour cream and a sprinkle of cheese for added richness.

Easy Comfort Beef Stew

Prep time: 15 minutes | Cook time: 8 hours | Serves 8

- 2 pounds (907 g) stewing beef, cubed
- 2 cups diced carrots
- 2 cups diced potatoes
- 2 medium onions, chopped
- 1 cup chopped celery
- 1 (10-ounce / 283-g) package lima beans
- 2 teaspoons quick-cooking tapioca
- 1 teaspoon salt
- ½ teaspoon pepper
- 1 (8-ounce / 227-g) can tomato sauce
- 1 cup water
- 1 tablespoon brown sugar

1. Place beef in bottom of crock pot. Add vegetables. 2. Sprinkle tapioca, salt, and pepper over ingredients. 3. Mix together tomato sauce and water. Pour over top. 4. Sprinkle brown sugar over all. 5. Cover. Cook on low 8 hours.

Mountain Bike Soup

Prep time: 10 minutes | Cook time: 2 to 6 hours | Serves 4

- 1 (12-ounce / 340-g) can chicken broth
- 1 (12-ounce / 340-g) can V-8 juice, regular or spicy
- ⅓ cup barley, rice, or broken
- spaghetti noodles, uncooked
- ⅓ cup chopped pepperoni, ham, or bacon
- 1 (15-ounce / 425-g) can cut green beans with liquid

1. Add all the ingredients to the crock pot, ensuring everything is evenly distributed. Put on the lid and set the crock pot to low.2. Enjoy a long bike ride for 2 to 6 hours while the dish slowly cooks to perfection. Return home to a delicious meal!

Rich and Creamy Tomato Soup

Prep time: 20 minutes | Cook time: 1½ hours | Serves 6

- 1 (26-ounce / 737-g) can condensed tomato soup, plus 6 ounces (170 g) water to equal 1 quart
- ½ teaspoon salt (optional)
- Half a stick butter
- 8 tablespoons flour
- 1 quart milk (whole or reduced-fat)

1. Put tomato soup, salt if you wish, and butter in crock pot. Blend well. 2. Cover and cook on high for 1 hour. 3. Meanwhile, place flour and 1 cup milk in 2-quart microwave-safe container. Whisk together until big lumps disappear. Then whisk in remaining milk until only small lumps remain. 4. Place flour-milk mixture in microwave and cook on high for 3 minutes. Remove and stir until smooth. Return to microwave and cook on high for another 3 minutes. 5. Add thickened milk slowly to hot soup in crock pot. 6. Heat thoroughly for 10 to 15 minutes.

Pacific Rim Pork and Noodle Soup

Prep time: 25 minutes | Cook time: 5 to 6 hours | Serves 8

- ½ cup soy sauce
- ¼ cup hoisin sauce
- ¼ cup rice wine
- Pinch five-spice powder
- 2 tablespoons toasted sesame oil
- 1 pork tenderloin (1¼ to 1½ pounds / 567 to 680 g), silver skin removed, cut into ½-inch slices
- 2 tablespoons vegetable oil
- 2 teaspoons freshly grated ginger
- 2 cloves garlic, minced
- 1 medium onion, coarsely chopped
- 1 bunch bok choy, cut into 1-inch pieces
- 2 medium carrots, cut into julienne strips
- 8 cups beef broth
- 8 ounces (227 g) fresh soba noodles, or 12 ounces (340 g) dried
- 4 green onions, finely chopped, using the white and tender green parts
- ¼ cup toasted sesame seeds, for garnish

1. In a large glass bowl, whisk together the soy sauce, hoisin, rice wine, five-spice powder, and sesame oil until smooth. Add the pork, ensuring it's well coated, then cover the bowl and refrigerate for at least 1 hour or up to 8 hours to allow the flavors to marinate.2. Heat the vegetable oil in a large skillet or wok over high heat. Remove the pork from the marinade and add it to the hot skillet, stir-frying in batches for 3 to 4 minutes until the pork is browned.3. Transfer the seared pork to the insert of a 5- to 7-quart crock pot. In the same skillet, add the ginger and garlic and stir-fry for about 1 minute, until fragrant. Add the onion, bok choy, and carrots, stir-

frying for 3 to 4 minutes until the vegetables are softened. Deglaze the skillet with 1 cup of broth, scraping up any browned bits from the pan.4. Pour the contents of the skillet into the crock pot. Add the remaining 7 cups of broth to the crock pot, then cover and cook on low for 4 to 5 hours, or until the pork and vegetables are tender.5. Stir in the noodles and green onions, cover, and continue cooking for an additional 45 minutes, until the noodles are cooked through.6. Serve the soup hot, garnished with toasted sesame seeds for added flavor and texture.

Sopranos-Style Sausage Minestrone

Prep time: 30 minutes | Cook time: 8 to 10 hours | Serves 8

- 1½ pounds (680 g) sweet Italian sausage, bulk or removed from casing
- 2 tablespoons extra-virgin olive oil
- 4 slices prosciutto, cut into julienne strips
- 2 medium onions, coarsely chopped
- 4 medium carrots, coarsely chopped
- 4 stalks celery with leaves, coarsely chopped
- 2 teaspoons finely chopped fresh rosemary
- ½ cup medium- to full-bodied red wine
- 1 (15-ounce / 425-g) can
- crushed plum tomatoes, with their juice
- 4 medium red potatoes, cut into ½-inch dice
- 4 ounces (113 g) green beans, ends snipped, cut into 1-inch lengths
- 2 medium zucchini, cut into ½-inch half rounds
- 1 cup dried brown lentils or split peas
- 1 head escarole or Swiss chard, cut into 1-inch pieces
- Rind from Parmigiano-Reggiano cheese, cut into ½-inch pieces (optional)
- 8 cups beef broth
- 2 cups cooked orzo

1. Begin by browning the sausage in a large skillet over high heat, breaking it apart as it cooks until it's fully browned and no longer pink.2. Once cooked, transfer the sausage to the insert of a 5- to 7-quart crock pot. Drain off most of the fat from the skillet, leaving only about 2 tablespoons, then add olive oil. Toss in the prosciutto and sauté for 2 minutes, letting it crisp up slightly.3. Add the onions, carrots, celery, and rosemary to the skillet, cooking for around 5 minutes until the onions soften. Pour in the wine to deglaze the pan, boiling it down until it's reduced by half, approximately 3 minutes. Stir in the tomatoes and let it simmer for 2 minutes to blend the flavors.4. Carefully transfer everything from the skillet into the crock pot. Add the potatoes, beans, zucchini, lentils, escarole, and the optional cheese rind. Pour in the broth, then cover the crock pot and let it cook on low for 8 to 10 hours, until the soup becomes thick and the lentils are tender.5. Stir in the orzo right before serving, ensuring everything is well combined, and enjoy the hearty soup.

Creamy Swiss Cheese Vegetable Soup

Prep time: 5 minutes | Cook time: 6 to 8 hours | Serves 4

- 2¼ cups frozen California-blend vegetables (broccoli, carrots, and cauliflower)
- ½ cup chopped onions
- ½ cup water
- ½ teaspoon chicken bouillon granules
- 1 cup skim milk
- 3 ounces (85 g) shredded fat-free Swiss cheese

1. Combine vegetables, onions, water, and bouillon in crock pot. 2. Cook on low 6 to 8 hours, or until vegetables are tender. 3. Pour into blender or food processor. Add milk. Process until smooth, or chunky smooth, whichever you prefer. 4. Serve, topped with shredded cheese.

Homemade Vegetable Stock

Prep time: 10 minutes | Cook time: 4 to 10 hours | Makes 6 cups

- 2 tomatoes, chopped
- 2 onions, cut up
- 4 carrots, cut up
- 1 stalk celery, cut up
- 1 potato, cut up
- 6 garlic cloves
- Dash of salt
- ½ teaspoon dried thyme
- 1 bay leaf
- 6 cups water

1. Combine tomatoes, onions, carrots, celery, potato, garlic, salt, thyme, bay leaf, and water. 2. Cover. Cook on low 8 to 10 hours, or on high 4 to 5 hours. 3. Strain stock through large sieve. Discard the solids. 4. Freeze until needed (up to 3 months). Use for soups or stews.

Turkey-Vegetable Stew

Prep time: 20 minutes | Cook time: 7 to 8 hours | Serves 6

- 3 tablespoons extra-virgin olive oil, divided
- 1 pound (454 g) boneless turkey breast, cut into 1-inch pieces
- 1 leek, thoroughly cleaned and sliced
- 2 teaspoons minced garlic
- 2 cups chicken broth
- 1 cup coconut milk
- 2 celery stalks, chopped
- 2 cups diced pumpkin
- 1 carrot, diced
- 2 teaspoons chopped thyme
- Salt, for seasoning
- Freshly ground black pepper, for seasoning
- 1 scallion, white and green parts, chopped, for garnish

1. Lightly grease the crock pot insert with 1 tablespoon of olive oil to prevent sticking.2. In a large skillet over medium-high heat, heat the remaining 2 tablespoons of olive oil. Add the turkey and sauté for about 5 minutes until browned.3. Add the leek and garlic to the skillet and sauté for another 3 minutes until softened and fragrant.4. Transfer the turkey mixture to the crock pot. Stir in the broth, coconut milk, celery, pumpkin, carrot, and thyme, ensuring everything is well mixed.5. Cover and cook on low for 7 to 8 hours, allowing the flavors to meld and the vegetables to become tender.6. Once done, season with salt and pepper to taste.7. Serve the dish topped with freshly chopped scallion for added flavor and color. Enjoy!

Hearty Lentil and Sausage Stew

Prep time: 10 minutes | Cook time: 4 to 6 hours | Serves 6

- 2 cups dry lentils, picked over and rinsed
- 1 (14½-ounce / 411-g) can diced tomatoes
- 8 cups canned chicken broth
- or water
- 1 tablespoon salt
- ½ to 1 pound (227 to 454 g) pork or beef sausage, cut into 2-inch pieces

1. In the crock pot, add the lentils, tomatoes, chicken broth, and salt, stirring to combine the ingredients evenly. Place the sausage pieces on top of the mixture.2. Cover the crock pot and cook on low for 4 to 6 hours, until the lentils are tender but not overcooked or mushy. Serve hot and enjoy!

Hearty Bean and Herb Soup

Prep time: 45 minutes | Cook time: 1 hour | Serves 6 to 8

- 1½ cups dry mixed beans
- 5 cups water
- 1 ham hock
- 1 cup chopped onions
- 1 cup chopped celery
- 1 cup chopped carrots
- 2 to 3 cups water
- 1 teaspoon salt
- ¼ to ½ teaspoon pepper
- 1 to 2 teaspoons fresh basil, or ½ teaspoon dried basil
- 1 to 2 teaspoons fresh oregano, or ½ teaspoon dried oregano
- 1 to 2 teaspoons fresh thyme, or ½ teaspoon dried thyme
- 2 cups fresh tomatoes, crushed, or 1 (14½-ounce / 411-g) can crushed tomatoes

1. Combine beans, water, and ham in saucepan. Bring to boil. Turn off heat and let stand 1 hour. 2. Combine onions, celery, and carrots in 2 to 3 cups water in another saucepan. Cook until soft. Mash slightly. 3. Combine all ingredients in crock pot. 4. Cover. Cook on high 2 hours, and then on low 2 hours.

Creamy Double Corn and Cheddar Chowder

Prep time: 10 minutes | Cook time: 4½ hours | Serves 6

- 1 tablespoon butter or margarine
- 1 cup onions, chopped
- 2 tablespoons all-purpose flour
- 2½ cups fat-free, reduced-sodium chicken broth
- 1 (16-ounce / 454-g) can creamed corn
- 1 cup frozen corn
- ½ cup finely chopped red bell peppers
- ½ teaspoon hot pepper sauce
- ¾ cup shredded, reduced-fat, sharp Cheddar cheese

1. In saucepan on top of stove, melt butter or margarine. Stir in onions and sauté until wilted. Stir in flour. When well mixed, whisk in chicken broth. Stir frequently over medium heat until broth is thickened. 2. Pour into crock pot. Mix in remaining ingredients except cheese. 3. Cook on low 4½ hours. About an hour before the end of the cooking time, stir in cheese until melted and well blended.

Five-Alarm Hill-o' -Beans Chili

Prep time: 30 minutes | Cook time: 8 to 10 hours | Serves 8 to 10

- 2 tablespoons olive oil
- 2 medium onions, coarsely chopped
- 2 cloves garlic, minced
- 2 jalapeño peppers, seeded and finely chopped
- 2 teaspoons ancho chile powder
- 1 teaspoon ground cumin
- 1 teaspoon dried oregano
- 2 medium red bell peppers, seeded and coarsely chopped
- 1 pound (454 g) cremini mushrooms, quartered
- 2 cups dried red beans, soaked, or 2 (14- to 15-ounce / 397- to 425-g) cans red beans, drained and rinsed
- 2 cups dried small white beans, soaked, or 2 (14- to
- 15-ounce / 397- to 425-g) cans white beans, drained and rinsed
- 2 cups dried pinto beans, soaked, or 2 (14- to 15-ounce / 397- to 425-g) cans pinto beans
- 1 (14- to 15-ounce / 397- to 425-g) can tomato purée
- 3 cups vegetable, chicken, or beef broth
- 1 (16-ounce / 454-g) package frozen corn, defrosted and drained
- Salt and freshly ground black pepper
- ½ cup finely chopped fresh cilantro
- Finely shredded Monterey Jack and Colby cheeses, for garnish
- Sour cream, for garnish

1. In a large skillet, heat the oil over medium-high heat. Add the onions, garlic, jalapeños, chili powder, cumin, and oregano, cooking for about 3 minutes until the onions soften and the spices become aromatic. 2. Transfer the sautéed mixture from the skillet to the insert of a 5- to 7-quart crock pot. Add the bell peppers, mushrooms, beans, tomato purée, broth, and corn. Stir well to ensure all the ingredients are evenly distributed. 3. Cover the crock pot and cook on low for 8 to 10 hours, allowing the flavors to blend together and the chili to thicken. 4. Once cooked, season with salt and pepper to taste, and stir in the fresh cilantro for a burst of flavor. Serve the chili hot, garnished with Monterey Jack cheese and a dollop of sour cream for added richness. Enjoy!

Flavorful Taco Chicken Soup

Prep time: 10 minutes | Cook time: 5 to 7 hours | Serves 4 to 6

- 1 envelope dry reduced-sodium taco seasoning
- 1 (32-ounce / 907-g) can low-sodium V-8 juice
- 1 (16-ounce / 454-g) jar salsa
- 1 (15-ounce / 425-g) can black beans
- 1 cup frozen corn
- 1 cup frozen peas
- 2 whole chicken breasts, cooked and shredded

1. Combine all ingredients except corn, peas, and chicken in crock pot. 2. Cover. Cook on low 4 to 6 hours. Add remaining vegetables and chicken 1 hour before serving.

Taco Soup with Pizza Sauce

Prep time: 15 minutes | Cook time: 3 to 4 hours | Serves 8 to 10

- 2 pounds (907 g) ground beef, browned
- 1 small onion, chopped and sautéed in ground beef drippings
- ¾ teaspoon salt
- ½ teaspoon pepper
- 1½ packages dry taco seasoning
- 1 quart pizza sauce
- 1 quart water
- Tortilla chips
- Shredded Mozzarella cheese
- Sour cream

1. In a 5-quart or larger crock pot, mix together the ground beef, onion, salt, pepper, taco seasoning, pizza sauce, and water, ensuring everything is well combined. 2. Cover the crock pot and cook on low for 3 to 4 hours, allowing the flavors to meld and the beef to cook through. 3. When ready to serve, top individual portions with tortilla chips, shredded cheese, and a dollop of sour cream for added texture and flavor. Enjoy!

Creamy Spiced Pumpkin Chicken Soup

Prep time: 15 minutes | Cook time: 6 hours | Serves 6

- 1 tablespoon extra-virgin olive oil
- 4 cups chicken broth
- 2 cups coconut milk
- 1 pound (454 g) pumpkin, diced
- ½ sweet onion, chopped
- 1 tablespoon grated fresh ginger
- 2 teaspoons minced garlic
- ½ teaspoon ground cinnamon
- ¼ teaspoon ground nutmeg
- ¼ teaspoon freshly ground black pepper
- ¼ teaspoon salt
- Pinch ground allspice
- 1 cup heavy (whipping) cream
- 2 cups chopped cooked chicken

1. Lightly grease the insert of the crock pot with the olive oil. 2. Place the broth, coconut milk, pumpkin, onion, ginger, garlic, cinnamon, nutmeg, pepper, salt, and allspice in the insert. 3. Cover and cook on low for 6 hours. 4. Using an immersion blender or a regular blender, purée the soup. 5. If you removed the soup from the insert to purée, add it back to the pot, and stir in the cream and chicken. 6. Keep heating the soup on low for 15 minutes to heat the chicken through, and then serve warm.

Italian Beef Stew

Prep time: 30 minutes | Cook time: 6 hours | Serves 4 to 6

- 2 tablespoons flour
- 2 teaspoons chopped fresh thyme
- 1 teaspoon salt
- ¼ to ½ teaspoon freshly ground pepper
- 2¼ pounds (1 kg) beef stewing meat, cubed
- 3 tablespoons olive oil
- 1 onion, chopped
- 1 cup tomato sauce
- 1 cup beef stock
- 1 cup red wine
- 3 garlic cloves, minced
- 2 tablespoons tomato paste
- 2 cups frozen peas, thawed but not cooked
- 1 teaspoon sugar

1. Place the flour in a small dish, then season it with thyme, salt, and pepper. Add the beef cubes to the dish, tossing them until they are evenly coated with the flour mixture.2. Heat the oil directly in the crock pot set on high. Once hot, add the floured beef cubes and brown them on all sides, ensuring a nice sear.3. Stir in all the remaining ingredients, except for the peas and sugar, ensuring everything is well mixed.4. Cover the crock pot and cook on low for 6 hours, allowing the flavors to develop and the beef to begin

tenderizing.5. After 6 hours, add the peas and sugar to the crock pot. Cover and cook for an additional 30 minutes, or until the beef is fully tender and the peas are warmed through. Serve hot.

Savory Hot and Sour Soup

Prep time: 10 minutes | Cook time: 4 to 12 hours | Serves 4

- 4 cups fat-free, low-sodium chicken broth
- 1 (8-ounce / 227-g) can sliced bamboo shoots, drained
- 1 carrot, julienned
- 1 (8-ounce / 227-g) can water chestnuts, drained and sliced
- 3 tablespoons quick-cooking tapioca
- 1 (6-ounce / 170-g) can sliced mushrooms, drained
- 1 tablespoon vinegar or rice
- wine vinegar
- 1 tablespoon light soy sauce
- 1 teaspoon sugar
- ¼ teaspoon black pepper
- ¼ to ½ teaspoon red pepper flakes, according to your taste preference
- 1 (8-ounce / 227-g) package frozen, peeled, and deveined shrimp (optional)
- 4 ounces (113 g) firm tofu, drained and cubed
- 1 egg, beaten

1. Combine all ingredients, except shrimp, tofu, and egg in crock pot. 2. Cover. Cook on low 9 to 11 hours, or on high 3 to 4 hours. 3. Add shrimp and tofu. 4. Cover. Cook 45 to 60 minutes. 5. Pour egg into the soup in a thin stream. Stir the soup gently until the egg forms fine shreds instead of clumps.

Zesty Mexican Tomato and Corn Soup

Prep time: 10 minutes | Cook time: 6 to 8 hours | Serves 8

- 1 medium onion, diced
- 1 medium green bell pepper, diced
- 1 clove garlic, minced
- 1 cup diced carrots
- 1 (14½-ounce / 411-g) can low-sodium diced Italian tomatoes
- 2½ cups low-sodium tomato juice
- 1 quart low-fat, low-sodium chicken broth
- 3 cups corn, frozen or canned
- 1 (4-ounce / 113-g) can chopped chilies, undrained
- 1 teaspoon chili powder
- 1½ teaspoons ground cumin
- Dash cayenne powder

1. Combine all ingredients in crock pot. 2. Cover. Cook on low 6 to 8 hours.

Turkey Carcass Broth

Prep time: 15 minutes | Cook time: 4 to 10 hours | Makes about 8 cups

- 1 turkey carcass, broken up into pieces
- 2 medium onions, coarsely chopped
- 3 medium carrots, coarsely chopped
- 3 medium stalks celery with leaves, coarsely chopped
- 8 cups chicken stock
- 2 teaspoons dried thyme
- 1 teaspoon dried sage leaves
- 1 bay leaf
- 4 whole black peppercorns
- Salt

1. Place all the ingredients, except the salt, into the insert of a 5- to 7-quart crock pot. Cover and cook on high for 4 to 5 hours, or on low for 8 to 10 hours, allowing the flavors to develop.2. Once cooked, season with salt to taste. Strain the broth through a colander to remove the large solids, then pass it through a fine mesh sieve for a smoother stock.3. Let the stock cool to room temperature, then transfer it to airtight containers. Store in the refrigerator for up to 5 days or in the freezer for up to 6 months for future use.

Hearty Southwestern Bean Soup with Cornmeal Dumplings

Prep time: 20 minutes | Cook time: 4½ to 12½ hours | Serves 4

Soup:
- 1 (15½-ounce / 439-g) can red kidney beans, rinsed and drained
- 1 (15½-ounce / 439-g) can black beans, pinto beans, or Great Northern beans, rinsed and drained
- 3 cups water
- 1 (14½-ounce / 411-g) can Mexican-style stewed tomatoes
- 1 (10-ounce / 283-g) package frozen whole-kernel corn, thawed
- 1 cup sliced carrots
- 1 cup chopped onions
- 1 (4-ounce / 113-g) can chopped green chilies
- 2 tablespoons instant beef, chicken, or vegetable bouillon granules
- 1 to 2 teaspoons chili powder
- 2 cloves garlic, minced

Dumplings:
- ⅓ cup flour
- ¼ cup yellow cornmeal
- 1 teaspoon baking powder
- Dash of salt
- Dash of pepper
- 1 egg white, beaten
- 2 tablespoons milk
- 1 tablespoon oil

1. Combine 11 soup ingredients in crock pot. 2. Cover. Cook on low 10 to 12 hours, or on high 4 to 5 hours. 3. Make dumplings by mixing together flour, cornmeal, baking powder, salt, and pepper.

4. Combine egg white, milk, and oil. Add to flour mixture. Stir with fork until just combined. 5. At the end of the soup's cooking time, turn crock pot to high. Drop dumpling mixture by rounded teaspoonfuls to make 8 mounds atop the soup. 6. Cover. Cook for 30 minutes (do not lift cover).

Pizza-Inspired Pasta Bowl

Prep time: 10 minutes | Cook time: 5 to 6 hours | Serves 6

- 1 (26-ounce / 737-g) jar fat-free, low-sodium marinara sauce
- 1 (14½-ounce / 411-g) can low-sodium diced tomatoes
- 4 ounces (113 g) low-fat pepperoni, diced or sliced
- 1½ cups fresh mushrooms, sliced
- 1 large bell pepper, diced
- 1 large red onion, chopped
- 1 cup water
- 1 tablespoon Italian seasoning
- 1 cup dry macaroni
- Low-fat shredded Mozzarella cheese

1. Combine all ingredients, except cheese, in cooker. 2. Cover. Cook on low 5 to 6 hours. 3. Ladle into soup bowls. Sprinkle with cheese.

Onion Soup

Prep time: 30 minutes | Cook time: 6 to 8 hours | Serves 8

- 3 medium onions, thinly sliced
- 2 tablespoons butter
- 2 tablespoons vegetable oil
- 1 teaspoon salt
- 1 tablespoon sugar
- 2 tablespoons flour
- 1 quart fat-free, low-sodium vegetable broth
- ½ cup dry white wine
- Slices of French bread
- ½ cup grated fat-free Swiss or Parmesan cheese

1. In a covered skillet, sauté the onions in butter and oil over medium heat until softened. Uncover the skillet, add the salt and sugar, and cook for an additional 15 minutes, stirring occasionally. Stir in the flour and cook for 3 more minutes to thicken.2. Transfer the onion mixture to the crock pot and combine it with the broth and wine.3. Cover the crock pot and cook on low for 6 to 8 hours, allowing the flavors to meld together.4. Toast slices of bread, sprinkle them with grated cheese, and broil until the cheese is melted and bubbly.5. Ladle the soup into individual bowls, then float a slice of broiled cheesy bread on top of each serving. Enjoy hot!

Jeanne's Vegetable-Beef Borscht

Prep time: 20 minutes | Cook time: 8 to 10 hours | Serves 8

- 1 pound (454 g) beef roast, cooked and cubed
- Half a head of cabbage, sliced thinly
- 3 medium potatoes, diced
- 4 carrots, sliced
- 1 large onion, diced
- 1 cup tomatoes, diced
- 1 cup corn
- 1 cup green beans
- 2 cups beef broth
- 2 cups tomato juice
- ¼ teaspoon garlic powder
- ¼ teaspoon dill seed
- 2 teaspoons salt
- ½ teaspoon pepper
- Water
- Sour cream
-

1. In the crock pot, combine all ingredients except the water and sour cream. Once mixed, add enough water to fill the crock pot about three-quarters full.2. Cover the crock pot and cook on low for 8 to 10 hours, allowing the flavors to develop.3. When ready to serve, top each individual serving with a dollop of sour cream. Enjoy!

Creamy Steak and Mushroom Soup

Prep time: 20 minutes | Cook time: 6 to 7 hours | Serves 6 to 8

- 4 tablespoons (½ stick) unsalted butter
- 1 cup finely chopped shallots (about 6 medium)
- 1½ pounds (680 g) assorted mushrooms, tougher stems removed, cut into ½-inch-thick slices
- 2½ teaspoons salt
- 1 teaspoon freshly ground black pepper
- 1½ teaspoons dried thyme

- leaves
- 2½ to 3 pounds (1.1 to 1.4 kg) beef top sirloin, cut into ½-inch pieces
- ¼ cup cream sherry
- 4 cups beef broth
- 2 tablespoons cornstarch mixed with ¼ cup water or broth
- 1 cup heavy cream
- ½ cup finely chopped fresh Italian parsley

1. Melt 2 tablespoons of the butter in a large skillet over medium-high heat. Add the shallots and mushrooms and sprinkle them with ½ teaspoon of the salt, ½ teaspoon of the pepper, and the thyme. Sauté until the mushrooms start to color, 10 to 15 minutes. 2. Transfer the mushrooms to the insert of a 5- to 7-quart crock pot. Sprinkle the meat with the remaining 2 teaspoons salt and ½ teaspoon pepper. 3. Melt the remaining 2 tablespoons butter in the skillet over high heat. Add the meat a few pieces at a time and brown on all sides. 4. Transfer the browned meat to the slow-cooker insert. Deglaze the pan with the sherry and scrape up any browned bits from the bottom of the skillet. 5. Transfer the sherry to the insert and stir in the broth. Cover and cook the soup on low for 5 to 6 hours, until the meat is tender. 6. Add the cornstarch mixture and the cream to the soup and stir to combine. Cook for an additional 30 minutes, until the soup is thickened. 7. Stir in the parsley before serving.

Caribbean-Style Black Bean Soup

Prep time: 10 minutes | Cook time: 4 to 10 hours | Serves 8 to 10

- 1 pound (454 g) dried black beans, washed and stones removed
- 3 onions, chopped
- 1 green pepper, chopped
- 4 coves garlic, minced
- 1 ham hock, or ¾ cup cubed ham
- 1 tablespoon oil
- 1 tablespoon ground cumin
- 2 teaspoons dried oregano
- 1 teaspoon dried thyme
- 1 tablespoon salt
- ½ teaspoon pepper
- 3 cups water
- 2 tablespoons vinegar
- Sour cream
- Fresh chopped cilantro

1. Soak the beans overnight in 4 quarts of water, then drain thoroughly.2. In the crock pot, combine the soaked beans, onions, green pepper, garlic, ham, oil, cumin, oregano, thyme, salt, pepper, and 3 cups of fresh water. Stir well to mix all the ingredients.3. Cover the crock pot and cook on low for 8 to 10 hours, or on high for 4 to 5 hours, until the beans are tender.4. For a thicker soup, remove half of the cooked bean mixture and purée it in a blender or mash it with a potato masher until smooth. Return the purée to the crock pot. If you prefer a thinner soup, skip this step.5. Stir in the vinegar. Debone the ham, cut it into bite-sized pieces, and return the ham to the soup.6. Serve the soup in bowls, topping each serving with a dollop of sour cream and a sprinkle of fresh cilantro. Enjoy!

Potato Soup with Possibilities

Prep time: 20 minutes | Cook time: 5 to 6 hours | Serves 6

- 5 cups homemade chicken broth, or 2 (14-ounce / 397-g) cans chicken broth, plus ½ soup can water
- 1 large onion, chopped
- 3 celery stalks, chopped,
- including leaves, if you like
- 6 large white potatoes, peeled, chopped, cubed, or sliced
- Salt and pepper to taste

1. Add all the ingredients into the crock pot, ensuring they are well mixed.2. Cover the crock pot and cook on high for 5 hours or on low for 6 hours, or until the vegetables are tender but still hold their shape without becoming mushy. Serve hot and enjoy!

Broccoli–Cheese with Noodles Soup

Prep time: 15 minutes | Cook time: 4 hours | Serves 8

- 2 cups noodles, cooked
- 1 (10-ounce / 283-g) package frozen chopped broccoli, thawed
- 3 tablespoons chopped onions
- 2 tablespoons butter
- 1 tablespoon flour
- 2 cups cubed processed cheese
- ½ teaspoon salt
- 5½ cups milk

1. In a saucepan, cook the noodles just until soft. While the noodles are cooking, combine the rest of the ingredients in the crock pot, mixing everything well.2. Once the noodles are cooked, drain them thoroughly and stir them into the mixture in the crock pot.3. Cover the crock pot and cook on low for 4 hours, allowing the flavors to meld. Serve hot and enjoy!

Hearty Split Pea and Ham Soup

Prep time: 15 minutes | Cook time: 4 hours | Serves 8

- 2½ quarts water
- 1 ham hock or pieces of cut-up ham
- 2½ cups split peas, dried
- 1 medium onion, chopped
- 3 medium carrots, cut in small pieces
- Salt and pepper to taste

1. Bring water to a boil in a saucepan on your stovetop. 2. Place all other ingredients into crock pot. Add water and stir together well. 3. Cover and cook on high for 4 hours, or until vegetables are tender. 4. If you've cooked a ham hock, remove it from the soup and debone the meat. Stir cut-up chunks of meat back into the soup before serving.

Green Bean and Ham Soup

Prep time: 15 minutes | Cook time: 4¼ to 6¼ hours | Serves 6

- 1 meaty ham bone, or 2 cups cubed ham
- 1½ quarts water
- 1 large onion, chopped
- 2 to 3 cups cut-up green beans
- 3 large carrots, sliced
- 2 large potatoes, peeled and cubed
- 1 tablespoon parsley
- 1 tablespoon summer savory
- ½ teaspoon salt
- ¼ teaspoon pepper
- 1 cup cream or milk

1. Add all the ingredients, except for the cream, to the crock pot and stir to combine.2. Cover the crock pot and cook on high for 4 to 6 hours, allowing the flavors to meld and the ingredients to cook thoroughly.3. Once done, remove the ham bone from the crock pot, cut off the meat, and return the meat to the crock pot.4. Turn the heat to low and stir in the cream or milk. Heat through until warm, then serve immediately.

Hearty Chicken and Pasta Soup

Prep time: 10 minutes | Cook time: 4 to 8 hours | Serves 6

- 6 boneless skinless chicken thighs
- 4 carrots, cut into 1-inch pieces
- 4 stalks celery, cut into ½-inch pieces
- 1 medium yellow onion, halved
- 2 garlic cloves, minced
- 2 bay leaves
- Sea salt
- Black pepper
- 6 cups chicken stock
- ½ cup small pasta like stelline or alphabet
- ¼ cup chopped fresh flat-leaf parsley

1. In the crock pot, place the chicken, carrots, celery, onion, and garlic. Add the bay leaves and season with salt and pepper. 2. Add the chicken stock. Cover and cook on high for 4 to 5 hours, or on low for 7 to 8 hours, until the chicken is cooked through and tender. 3. About 20 minutes before serving, transfer the chicken to a bowl. Let the chicken cool until it can comfortably be handled. 4. Remove and discard the onion and bay leaves. If the crock pot is on the low setting, turn it to high. 5. Add the pasta to the crock pot, cover, and cook until tender, 15 to 18 minutes. 6. Meanwhile, shred the chicken. 7. Stir the chicken into the soup along with the parsley. When the chicken is heated through, about 5 minutes, serve the soup hot.

Hearty Barley and Cabbage Soup

Prep time: 15 minutes | Cook time: 5 to 12 hours | Serves 8

- ¼ cup dry pearl barley
- 6 cups fat-free, low-sodium meat or vegetable broth
- 1 cup chopped onions
- 3 to 4 cups finely chopped green cabbage
- ¼ cup chopped fresh parsley
- ½ teaspoon celery salt
- ½ teaspoon salt
- ⅛ teaspoon black pepper
- 1 tablespoon minute tapioca

1. Combine all ingredients in crock pot. 2. Cover. Cook on low 10 to 12 hours, or on high 5 to 6 hours.

Classic Beef and Barley Soup

Prep time: 20 minutes | Cook time: 6 to 7 hours | Serves 8

- 2½ to 3 pounds (1.1 to 1.4 kg) beef chuck, sirloin, or flap meat, cut into ½-inch pieces
- Salt and freshly ground black pepper
- 2 tablespoons extra-virgin olive oil
- 2 cloves garlic, minced
- 2 medium onions, coarsely chopped
- 8 ounces (227 g) cremini mushrooms, quartered
- 1½ teaspoons dried thyme
- 4 medium carrots, coarsely chopped
- 3 stalks celery with leaves, coarsely chopped
- 3 tablespoons tomato paste
- 1 cup medium- to full-bodied red wine, such as Merlot, Chianti, Barolo, or Cabernet
- 6 cups beef broth
- ½ cup pearl barley

1. Sprinkle the beef evenly with the 2 teaspoons salt and 1 teaspoon pepper. Heat the oil in a large skillet over high heat. Add the meat a few pieces at a time and brown on all sides. Transfer the browned meat to the insert of a 5- to 7-quart crock pot. 2. Add the garlic, onions, mushrooms, and thyme to the same skillet over medium-high heat and sauté until the liquid from the mushrooms is evaporated. 3. Transfer the contents of the skillet to the slow-cooker insert. Add the carrots and celery to the cooker and stir to combine. Deglaze the skillet with the tomato paste and wine and allow the wine to reduce by about ¼ cup, stirring up any browned bits from the bottom of the pan. 4. Transfer the tomato mixture to the slow-cooker insert and add the broth and barley. Cover the crock pot and cook on low for 6 to 7 hours, until the beef and barley are tender. 5. Season with salt and pepper before serving.

Thai Chicken–Coconut Soup

Prep time: 15 minutes | Cook time: 8 hours | Serves 2

- 5 boneless, skinless chicken thighs
- 1 cup sliced shiitake or cremini mushrooms
- 2 garlic cloves, minced
- 2 teaspoons grated fresh ginger
- ½ teaspoon lime zest
- 2 cups chicken stock
- 1 cup coconut milk
- 1 tablespoon freshly squeezed lime juice
- 1 tablespoon Thai fish sauce
- 1 teaspoon curry powder
- 1 cup fresh snap peas
- ½ red bell pepper, cut with spiral cutter, if desired
- ¼ cucumber, cut with spiral cutter, if desired

1. In the crock pot, combine all the ingredients except for the snap peas, red bell pepper, and cucumber. Stir to ensure everything is well mixed. 2. Cover the crock pot and cook on low for 7½ hours, or until the chicken is tender and fully cooked. 3. Once the chicken is tender, remove it from the soup and shred it into bite-sized pieces. Return the shredded chicken to the crock pot and stir. 4. Add the snap peas to the crock pot, cover, and cook on low for an additional 20 minutes, until the snap peas are crisp-tender. 5. Ladle the soup into two bowls and serve hot. Garnish with the spiral-cut red bell pepper and cucumber for added freshness and color. Enjoy!

Hearty Green Chili and Meat Stew

Prep time: 20 minutes | Cook time: 4 to 6 hours | Serves 6 to 8

- 3 tablespoons oil
- 2 garlic cloves, minced
- 1 large onion, diced
- 1 pound (454 g) ground sirloin
- ½ pound (227 g) ground pork
- 3 cups chicken broth
- 2 cups water
- 2 (4-ounce / 113-g) cans diced green chilies
- 4 large potatoes, diced
- 1 (10-ounce / 283-g) package frozen corn
- 1 teaspoon black pepper
- 1 teaspoon crushed dried oregano
- ½ teaspoon ground cumin
- 1 teaspoon salt

1. Brown onion, garlic, sirloin, and pork in oil in skillet. Cook until meat is no longer pink. 2. Combine all ingredients in crock pot. 3. Cover. Cook on low 4 to 6 hours, or until potatoes are soft.

Creamy Cheddar Cheese Soup

Prep time: 15 minutes | Cook time: 6 hours | Serves 6

- 1 tablespoon butter
- 5 cups chicken broth
- 1 cup coconut milk
- 2 celery stalks, chopped
- 1 carrot, chopped
- ½ sweet onion, chopped
- Pinch cayenne pepper
- 8 ounces (227 g) cream
- cheese, cubed
- 2 cups shredded Cheddar cheese
- Salt, for seasoning
- Freshly ground black pepper, for seasoning
- 1 tablespoon chopped fresh thyme, for garnish

1. Lightly grease the insert of the crock pot with the butter. 2. Place the broth, coconut milk, celery, carrot, onion, and cayenne pepper in the insert. 3. Cover and cook on low for 6 hours. 4. Stir in the cream cheese and Cheddar, then season with salt and pepper. 5. Serve topped with the thyme.

Moroccan-Style Chicken Vegetable Soup with Couscous

Prep time: 20 minutes | Cook time: 6 hours | Serves 8

- 2 tablespoons olive oil
- 1 medium onion, finely chopped
- 1 teaspoon ground cumin
- 1 teaspoon sweet paprika
- ¼ teaspoon ground cinnamon
- Pinch of cayenne pepper
- 2 medium zucchini, diced
- 2 medium yellow squash, diced
- 1 (14- to 15-ounce / 397- to 425-g) can diced tomatoes, with their juice
- 6 cups chicken broth
- 3 cups shredded cooked chicken
- ½ cup golden raisins
- 3 cups cooked couscous

1. Heat the oil in a large skillet over medium-high heat. 2. Add the onion, cumin, paprika, cinnamon, and cayenne and sauté until the onion begins to soften, about 3 minutes. Add the zucchini, squash, and tomatoes and toss to coat with the spices and onion. 3. Transfer the contents of the skillet to the insert of a 5- to 7-quart crock pot. Stir in the broth, chicken, and raisins. 4. Cover and cook on low for 6 hours, until the chicken and vegetables are tender. 5. Serve the soup over couscous in individual bowls.

Best Everyday Stew

Prep time: 20 minutes | Cook time: 10 hours | Serves 8

- 2¼ pounds (1 kg) flank steak, 1½-inch thick
- 8 red potatoes, small to medium in size
- 10 baby carrots
- 1 large clove garlic, diced
- 1 medium to large onion, chopped
- 1 cup baby peas
- 3 ribs celery, cut in 1-inch pieces
- 3 cups cabbage, in chunks
- 2 (8-ounce / 227-g) cans low-sodium tomato sauce
- 1 tablespoon Worcestershire
- sauce
- 2 bay leaves
- ¼ to ½ teaspoon dried thyme, according to your taste preference
- ¼ to ½ teaspoon dried basil, according to your taste preference
- ¼ to ½ teaspoon dried marjoram, according to your taste preference
- 1 tablespoon parsley
- 2 cups water or more, if desired
- 4 cubes beef or vegetable bouillon

1. Trim the flank steak, removing any excess fat, and cut it into 1½-inch cubes.2. In a nonstick skillet, slowly brown the steak on all sides. Quarter the potatoes while the steak browns.3. Transfer the browned steak, quartered potatoes, and all remaining ingredients into a large crock pot, stirring to combine.4. Cover the crock pot

and cook on high for 1 hour. Afterward, turn the heat to low and cook for an additional 9 hours, allowing the flavors to blend and the meat to become tender. Serve hot and enjoy!

Comforting Chicken Noodle Soup

Prep time: 15 minutes | Cook time: 4 to 8 hours | Serves 8 to 10

- 2 tablespoons olive oil
- 1 cup finely chopped onion
- 2 cups finely chopped celery
- 2 cups finely chopped carrot
- 2 small zucchini, finely chopped
- 1 teaspoon dried thyme
- 12 cups chicken broth
- 4 cups bite-size pieces cooked chicken
- 2 (10-ounce / 283-g) packages fresh baby spinach
- Salt and freshly ground black pepper
- 8 ounces (227 g) medium-width egg noodles, cooked al dente

1. Heat the oil in a large skillet over medium-high heat. Add the onion, celery, carrot, zucchini, and thyme and sauté until the vegetables are softened, about 7 minutes. 2. Transfer the contents of the skillet to the insert of a 5- to 7-quart crock pot. Stir in the broth, chicken, and spinach. 3. Cover and cook on high for 4 hours or on low for 8 hours. 4. Season with salt and pepper. Add the noodles to the soup, stir, cover, and let stand for 5 minutes before serving.

Mexican Rice and Bean Soup

Prep time: 15 minutes | Cook time: 6 hours | Serves 6

- ½ cup chopped onions
- ⅓ cup chopped green peppers
- 1 garlic clove, minced
- 1 tablespoon oil
- 1 (4-ounce / 113-g) package sliced or chipped dried beef
- 1 (18-ounce / 510-g) can tomato juice
- 1 (15½-ounce / 439-g) can
- red kidney beans, undrained
- 1½ cups water
- ½ cup long-grain rice, uncooked
- 1 teaspoon paprika
- ½ to 1 teaspoon chili powder
- ½ teaspoon salt
- Dash of pepper

1. In a skillet, cook the onions, green peppers, and garlic in oil over medium heat until the vegetables are tender but not browned. Transfer the cooked vegetables to the crock pot.2. Tear the beef into small pieces and add them to the crock pot along with the vegetables.3. Add the remaining ingredients to the crock pot and mix everything well to combine.4. Cover and cook on low for 6 hours, allowing the flavors to blend. Stir the mixture before serving.5. Serve hot and enjoy!

Spanish Vegetable Stew

- 2 tablespoons olive oil
- 3 shallots, chopped
- 1 large carrot, sliced
- 2 garlic cloves, minced
- 1 pound (454 g) red potatoes, quartered
- 1 red bell pepper, chopped
- 1 (9-ounce / 255-g) package quartered artichoke hearts
- 1 (15-ounce / 425-g) can diced tomatoes with the juice
- 1½ cups cooked chickpeas
- ⅓ cup dry white wine
- 1½ cups vegetable stock
- 1 teaspoon minced fresh thyme leaves (or ½ teaspoon dried)
- 1 teaspoon minced fresh oregano leaves (or ½ teaspoon dried)
- 1 large bay leaf
- Sea salt
- Black pepper

1. Heat the oil in a large skillet over medium heat. Add the shallots, carrot, and garlic, stirring frequently, and cook until the vegetables are softened, about 8 minutes. Transfer the cooked vegetables to the crock pot. 2. Add the potatoes, bell pepper, artichoke hearts, tomatoes, chickpeas, wine, and stock into the crock pot with the vegetables. 3. Sprinkle in the thyme, oregano, and bay leaf, then season with salt and pepper to taste. Cover the crock pot and cook on low for 6 to 8 hours, allowing the flavors to meld together. Serve hot and enjoy!

Hearty Sunday Chicken Stew with Dumplings

- ½ cup all-purpose flour
- 1 teaspoon salt
- ½ teaspoon white pepper
- 1 (3-pound / 1.4-kg) broiler/fryer chicken, cut up and skin removed
- 2 tablespoons canola oil
- 3 cups chicken broth

Dumplings:
- 1 cup all-purpose flour
- 2 teaspoons baking powder
- ½ teaspoon salt

- 6 large carrots, cut into 1-inch pieces
- 2 celery ribs, cut into ½-inch pieces
- 1 large sweet onion, thinly sliced
- 1 teaspoon dried rosemary, crushed
- 1½ cups frozen peas

- ½ teaspoon dried rosemary, crushed
- 1 egg, lightly beaten
- ½ cup 2% milk

1. In a large resealable plastic bag, combine the flour, salt and pepper; add chicken, a few pieces at a time, and shake to coat. In a large skillet, brown chicken in oil; remove and keep warm. Gradually add broth to the skillet; bring to a boil. 2. In a 5-quart crock pot, layer carrots, celery and onion; sprinkle with rosemary. Add the chicken and hot broth. Cover and cook on low for 6 to 8 hours or until chicken and vegetables are tender and stew is bubbling. 3. Remove chicken; when cool enough to handle, remove meat from the bones and discard bones. Cut meat into bite-size pieces and return to the crock pot. Stir in peas. 4. For dumplings, in a small bowl, combine the flour, baking powder, salt and rosemary. Combine the egg and milk; stir into dry ingredients. Drop by heaping teaspoonfuls onto simmering chicken mixture. Cover and cook on high for 25 to 30 minutes or until a toothpick inserted in a dumpling comes out clean (do not lift the cover while simmering).

Monterey Bay Spicy Bean Soup with Tortilla Strips

- ⅓ cup vegetable oil
- 1 large onion, finely chopped
- 1 clove garlic, minced
- 4 Anaheim chiles, seeded and chopped
- 1½ teaspoons chili powder
- 1 (14- to 15-ounce / 397- to 425-g) can chopped tomatoes, drained
- 2 (14- to 15-ounce / 397- to 425-g) cans pinto beans, drained and rinsed
- 6 cups chicken broth
- 2 cups cooked chorizo

- sausage, crumbled (optional)
- Salt and freshly ground black pepper
- 2 cups broken fried tortilla strips
- ½ cup shredded mild Cheddar or Monterey Jack cheese
- ½ cup sour cream, for garnish
- 4 green onions, chopped, using the white and tender green parts, for garnish
- ½ cup finely minced fresh cilantro, for garnish

1. Heat the oil in a large skillet over medium heat. Add the onion, garlic, and chiles and sauté until the vegetables are softened, about 5 minutes. Stir in the chili powder and cook, stirring, for about 1 minute, until fragrant. 2. Transfer the contents of the skillet to the insert of a 5- to 7-quart crock pot. Add the tomatoes, beans, broth, and sausage (if using). 3. Cover the crock pot and cook the soup on high for 3 to 4 hours or on low for 7 to 8 hours. 4. Season with salt and pepper. Add the tortilla strips to the soup, cover, and let stand for 10 minutes, until the strips just begin to soften. 5. Divide the cheese among 8 bowls and ladle the soup over. 6. Garnish each serving with a dollop of sour cream, chopped green onion, and minced cilantro.

Mariner's Delight Shellfish Stew

- ¼ cup extra-virgin olive oil
- 1 medium onion, finely chopped
- 3 cloves garlic, minced
- 1 medium green bell pepper, seeded and finely chopped
- 1½ teaspoons dried oregano
- 1½ teaspoons dried basil
- ⅛ teaspoon red pepper flakes
- 1½ cups white wine
- 1 (28- to 32-ounce / 794- to 907-g) can plum tomatoes, drained and chopped
- 3 tablespoons tomato paste
- 1 (8-ounce / 227-g) bottle clam juice
- 1 bay leaf
- ½ teaspoon freshly ground black pepper
- 1 large Dungeness crab or 4 large king crab legs, cracked and cut into bite-size pieces
- 2 lobster tails, split and cut into 1-inch chunks
- 1 pound (454 g) sea bass, cut into 1-inch chunks
- ¾ pound (340 g) medium shrimp, peeled and deveined
- 24 littleneck clams, shells scrubbed
- ½ cup finely chopped fresh Italian parsley, for garnish

1. Heat the oil in a large skillet over medium-high heat. Add the onion, garlic, bell pepper, oregano, basil, and red pepper flakes and sauté until the onion is softened, about 3 minutes. Deglaze the pan with the wine, scraping up any browned bits from the bottom of the pan, and bring to a boil. Reduce by half. 2. Transfer the contents of the skillet to the insert of a 5- to 7-quart crock pot. Stir in the tomatoes, tomato paste, clam juice, bay leaf, and pepper. Cover and cook on low for 5 hours. Add the crab, lobster, sea bass, shrimp, and clams. 3. Cover and cook on low for 1 hour, until the shrimp are pink and the clams have opened. Discard the bay leaf and any clams that have not opened. Carefully stir the stew, being careful not to break up the sea bass chunks. 4. Serve the stew garnished with the parsley.

Zesty Taco Soup

- 1 pound (454 g) ground beef
- 1 large onion, chopped
- 1 (16-ounce / 454-g) can Mexican-style tomatoes
- 1 (16-ounce / 454-g) can ranch-style beans
- 1 (16-ounce / 454-g) can whole-kernel corn, undrained
- 1 (16-ounce / 454-g) can kidney beans, undrained
- 1 (16-ounce / 454-g) can black beans, undrained
- 1 (16-ounce / 454-g) jar picante sauce
- Corn or tortilla chips
- Sour cream
- Shredded Cheddar cheese

1. In a skillet, brown the meat and onions together, then drain any excess fat.2. Transfer the browned meat and onions to the crock pot and combine with all the other vegetables and picante sauce, stirring to mix well.3. Cover the crock pot and cook on low for 4 to 6 hours, allowing the flavors to meld.4. Serve the dish with corn or tortilla chips, and top with sour cream and shredded cheese for added flavor. Enjoy!

White Bean and Barley Soup

- 1 large onion, chopped
- 2 garlic cloves, minced
- 1 tablespoon olive or canola oil
- 2 (24-ounce / 680-g) cans Great Northern beans, undrained
- 4 cups no-fat, low-sodium chicken broth
- 4 cups water
- 2 large carrots, chunked
- 2 medium green or red bell peppers, chunked
- 2 celery ribs, chunked
- ½ cup quick-cooking barley
- ¼ cup chopped fresh parsley
- 2 bay leaves
- ½ teaspoon dried thyme
- ¼ teaspoon black pepper
- 1 (28-ounce / 794-g) can diced tomatoes, undrained

1. In a skillet, sauté the onion and garlic in oil over medium heat until they are just wilted.2. Transfer the sautéed onion and garlic to the crock pot, and combine with all the remaining ingredients.3. Cover the crock pot and cook on low for 8 to 10 hours, allowing the flavors to develop.4. Before serving, be sure to discard the bay leaves. Serve hot and enjoy!

Hearty Sweet Potato and Lentil Stew

- 4 cups fat-free vegetable broth
- 3 cups sweet potatoes, peeled and cubed
- 1½ cups lentils, rinsed
- 3 medium carrots, cut into 1-inch pieces
- 1 medium onion, chopped
- 4 garlic cloves, minced
- ½ teaspoon ground cumin
- ¼ teaspoon ground ginger
- ¼ teaspoon cayenne pepper
- ¼ cup minced fresh cilantro or parsley
- ¼ teaspoon salt

1. Combine first nine ingredients in crock pot. 2. Cook on low 5 to 6 hours or just until vegetables are tender. 3. Stir in cilantro and salt just before serving.

Beef ' n Black Bean Soup

- 1 pound (454 g) extra-lean ground beef
- 2 (14½-ounce / 411-g) cans fat-free, low-sodium chicken broth
- 1 (14½-ounce / 411-g) can low-sodium, diced tomatoes, undrained
- 8 green onions, thinly sliced
- 3 medium carrots, thinly sliced
- 2 celery ribs, thinly sliced
- 2 garlic cloves, minced
- 1 tablespoon sugar
- 1½ teaspoons dried basil
- ½ teaspoon salt
- ½ teaspoon dried oregano
- ½ teaspoon ground cumin
- ½ teaspoon chili powder
- 2 (15-ounce / 425-g) cans black beans, rinsed and drained
- 1½ cups rice, cooked

1. In a nonstick skillet over medium heat, cook the beef until it is no longer pink, then drain any excess fat.2. Transfer the cooked beef to the crock pot.3. Add all the remaining ingredients to the crock pot, except for the black beans and rice. Stir to combine.4. Cover the crock pot and cook on high for 1 hour.5. After 1 hour, reduce the heat to low and cook for an additional 4 to 5 hours, or until the vegetables are tender.6. Stir in the black beans and rice.7. Continue cooking on low for 1 more hour, or until everything is heated through. Serve hot and enjoy!

Green Bean and Sausage Soup

- 1 medium onion, chopped
- 2 carrots, sliced
- 2 ribs celery, sliced
- 1 tablespoon olive oil
- 5 medium potatoes, cubed
- 1 (10-ounce / 283-g) package frozen green beans
- 2 (14½-ounce / 411-g) cans chicken broth
- 2 broth cans water
- ⅓ pound (151 g) link sausage, sliced, or bulk sausage, browned
- 2 tablespoons chopped fresh parsley, or 2 teaspoons dried
- 1 to 2 tablespoons chopped fresh oregano, or 1 to 2 teaspoons dried
- 1 teaspoon Italian spice
- Salt to taste
- Pepper to taste

1. In a skillet, sauté the onion, carrots, and celery in oil over medium heat until they become tender.2. Transfer the sautéed vegetables to the crock pot and combine with all the remaining ingredients, stirring well to mix.3. Cover the crock pot and cook on high for 1 to 2 hours, then reduce the heat to low and cook for an additional 6 to 8 hours.4. Serve hot and enjoy!

Chapter 7
Snacks and Appetizers

Chapter 7 Snacks and Appetizers

Savory Roasted Tomato & Mozzarella Topping

Prep time: 15 minutes | Cook time: 5 hours | Serves 8

- ¼ cup extra-virgin olive oil
- 1 large red onion, coarsely chopped
- 2 teaspoons dried basil
- 1 teaspoon fresh rosemary leaves, finely chopped
- 4 cloves garlic, minced
- 3 (28- to 32-ounce / 794-

- to 907-g) cans whole plum tomatoes, drained
- 2 teaspoons salt
- ⅛ teaspoon red pepper flakes
- 8 ounces (227 g) fresh Mozzarella, cut into ½-inch dice

1. Lightly toasted baguette slices for serving 2. Combine all the ingredients except the Mozzarella and the baguette slices in the insert of a 5- to 7-quart crock pot. Cover and cook on high for 2 hours. Uncover the cooker and cook on low, stirring occasionally, for 3 hours, until the tomato liquid has almost evaporated. 3. Remove the tomato mixture to the bowl of a food processor and pulse on and off five times to chop the tomatoes and garlic. Transfer to a serving bowl to cool, then stir in the Mozzarella. 4. Serve with the toasted baguette slices.

Cheesy Italian Tomato Fondue

Prep time: 15 minutes | Cook time: 1 hour | Serves 4 to 6

- 1 (1-pound / 454-g) block of cheese, your choice of good melting cheese, cut in ½-inch cubes
- 2 cups shredded Mozzarella cheese

- 1 (19-ounce / 539-g) can Italian-style stewed tomatoes with juice
- Loaf of Italian bread, slices toasted and then cut into 1-inch cubes

1. Place cheese cubes, shredded Mozzarella cheese, and tomatoes in a lightly greased crock pot. 2. Cover and cook on high 45 to 60 minutes, or until cheese is melted. 3. Stir occasionally and scrape down sides of crock pot with rubber spatula to prevent scorching. 4. Reduce heat to low and serve. (Fondue will keep a smooth consistency for up to 4 hours.) 5. Serve with toasted bread cubes for dipping.

Sweet and Spicy Peanuts

Prep time: 10 minutes | Cook time: 1½ hours | Makes 4 cups

- 3 cups salted peanuts
- ½ cup sugar
- ⅓ cup packed brown sugar
- 2 tablespoons hot water

- 2 tablespoons butter, melted
- 1 tablespoon Sriracha Asian hot chili sauce or hot pepper sauce
- 1 teaspoon chili powder

1. Add the peanuts to a greased 1½-quart crock pot. In a small bowl, mix together the sugars, water, butter, hot sauce, and chili powder until well combined. Pour this mixture over the peanuts in the crock pot.2. Cover the crock pot and cook on high for 1½ hours, stirring once during cooking to ensure the peanuts are evenly coated.3. Once cooked, spread the peanuts out on waxed paper to cool completely. Once cooled, store them in an airtight container for later enjoyment.

Snack Mix

Prep time: 10 minutes | Cook time: 2 hours | Serves 10 to 14

- 8 cups Chex cereal, of any combination
- 6 cups pretzels
- 6 tablespoons butter, melted
- 2 tablespoons

- Worcestershire sauce
- 1 teaspoon seasoned salt
- ½ teaspoon garlic powder
- ½ teaspoon onion salt
- ½ teaspoon onion powder

1. In the crock pot, combine the first two ingredients and stir until evenly mixed.2. In a separate bowl, combine the melted butter and seasonings. Pour this mixture over the dry ingredients in the crock pot, tossing everything together until well coated.3. Cover the crock pot and cook on low for 2 hours, stirring every 30 minutes to ensure even cooking. Serve hot and enjoy!

Spiced Curry Almonds

- 2 tablespoons butter, melted
- 1 tablespoon curry powder
- ½ teaspoon seasoned salt
- 1 pound (454 g) blanched almonds

1. Combine butter with curry powder and seasoned salt. 2. Pour over almonds in crock pot. Mix to coat well. 3. Cover. Cook on low 2 to 3 hours. Turn to high. Uncover cooker and cook 1 to 1½ hours. 4. Serve hot or cold.

Hot Dill and Swiss Dip

- 2 medium sweet onions, such as Vidalia, finely chopped
- 2 tablespoons finely chopped fresh dill
- 1½ cups mayonnaise
- 2 cups finely shredded Havarti with dill
- 2 cups finely shredded Swiss cheese

1. Lightly coat the insert of a 1½- to 3-quart crock pot with nonstick cooking spray to prevent sticking. In a mixing bowl, combine all the ingredients thoroughly, then transfer the mixture into the crock pot. Cover the pot with the lid and cook on low for 2 to 3 hours, or until the mixture is bubbling. 2. Once cooked, serve the dish directly from the crock pot, keeping it set on warm to maintain temperature. Enjoy your meal!

Sweet & Savory BBQ Bites

- 1 pound (454 g) ground beef
- ¼ cup finely chopped onion
- 1 (16-ounce / 454-g) package miniature hot dogs, drained
- 1 (12-ounce / 340-g) jar apricot preserves
- 1 cup barbecue sauce
- 1 (20-ounce / 567-g) can pineapple chunks, drained

1. In a large bowl, combine beef and onion, mixing lightly but thoroughly. Shape into 1-inch balls. In a large skillet over medium heat, cook meatballs in two batches until cooked through, turning occasionally. 2. Using a slotted spoon, transfer meatballs to a 3-quart crock pot. Add the hot dogs; stir in the preserves and barbecue sauce. Cook, covered, on high 2 to 3 hours or until heated through. 3. Stir in the pineapple; cook, covered, 15 to 20 minutes longer or until mixture is heated through.

Slow Cooked Smokies

- 2 pounds (907 g) miniature smoked sausage links
- 1 (28-ounce / 794-g) bottle barbecue sauce
- 1¼ cups water
- 3 tablespoons Worcestershire sauce
- 3 tablespoons steak sauce
- ½ teaspoon pepper

1. In the crock pot, add all the ingredients and mix them thoroughly until well combined. 2. Cover the crock pot and cook on low for 6 to 7 hours, allowing the flavors to meld and the dish to cook through. Serve hot and enjoy!

Creamy Clam Delight Dip

- 2 (8-ounce / 227-g) packages cream cheese at room temperature and cut into cubes
- ½ cup mayonnaise
- 3 green onions, finely chopped, using the white and tender green parts
- 2 cloves garlic, minced
- 3 (8-ounce / 227-g) cans minced or chopped clams, drained with ¼ cup clam juice reserved
- 1 tablespoon Worcestershire sauce
- 2 teaspoons anchovy paste
- ¼ cup finely chopped fresh Italian parsley

1. Coat the insert of a 1½- to 3-quart crock pot with nonstick cooking spray. Combine all the ingredients in a large mixing bowl, adding the clam juice to thin the dip. 2. Transfer the mixture to the crock pot, cover, and cook on low for 2 to 3 hours, until bubbling. 3. Serve from the cooker set on warm.

Meaty Buffet Favorites

- 1 cup tomato sauce
- 1 teaspoon Worcestershire sauce
- ½ teaspoon prepared
- mustard
- 2 tablespoons brown sugar
- 1 pound (454 g) prepared meatballs or mini-wieners

1. In the crock pot, combine the first four ingredients and mix them well. 2. Add the meatballs or mini-wieners, stirring gently to coat them in the mixture. 3. Cover the crock pot and cook on high for 2 hours. After that, turn the heat to low. Serve the dish as an appetizer directly from the crock pot. Enjoy!

Sweet and Spicy Mustard Dogs

Prep time: 15 minutes | Cook time: 1 to 2 hours | Serves 12

- 12 hot dogs, cut into bite-size pieces
- 1 cup grape jelly
- 1 cup prepared mustard

1. Place all ingredients in crock pot. Stir well. 2. Turn on high until mixture boils. Stir. 3. Turn to low and bring to the buffet table.

Creamy Cranberry Meatballs

Prep time: 15 minutes | Cook time: 2 to 6 hours | Serves 6

- 50 meatballs, about 1½ pounds (680 g)
- 1 cup brown gravy, from a jar, or made from a mix
- 1 cup whole-berry cranberry sauce
- 2 tablespoons heavy cream
- 2 teaspoons Dijon mustard

1. Place the meatballs in the crock pot, ensuring they are evenly distributed. 2. In a separate bowl, mix together all the remaining ingredients until well combined. Pour this mixture over the meatballs, making sure they are thoroughly coated. 3. Cover the crock pot and cook on high for 2 to 3 hours, or on low for 5 to 6 hours, allowing the flavors to meld and the meatballs to cook through. Serve hot and enjoy!

Orange Chipotle Wings

Prep time: 15 minutes | Cook time: 3 hours | Serves 8

- 3 pounds (1.4 kg) chicken wing drumettes
- 1 medium red onion, finely chopped
- 6 chipotle chiles in adobo, finely chopped
- 1 teaspoon ground cumin
- 2 cloves garlic, minced
- 1½ cups orange juice
- ½ cup honey
- ½ cup ketchup
- ½ cup finely chopped fresh cilantro

1. Lightly spray the insert of a 5- to 7-quart crock pot with nonstick cooking spray to prepare it. 2. Place the wings on a rack set in a baking sheet and broil them until one side is crispy and golden brown. 3. Flip the wings over and broil the other side for an additional 5 minutes until crispy and browned. 4. Once done, take the wings out of the oven. If you want to prepare this step in advance, let the wings cool and store them in the refrigerator for up to 2 days; otherwise, transfer the wings to the prepared crock pot insert. 5. In a mixing bowl, combine the remaining ingredients and pour the mixture over the wings, making sure to turn the wings to coat them well with the sauce. 6. Cover the crock pot and cook the wings on high for 3 hours, turning them twice during cooking to ensure they are evenly cooked. 7. Once cooked, serve the wings straight from the crock pot, keeping it set on warm for guests to enjoy.

Zesty Refried Bean and Sausage Dip

Prep time: 20 minutes | Cook time: 2 to 3 hours | Serves 8

- 8 ounces (227 g) spicy sausages, such as chorizo, andouille, or Italian, removed from its casing
- 1 medium onion, chopped
- 2 Anaheim chiles, seeded and chopped
- 1 medium red or yellow bell pepper, seeded and chopped
- 2 (14- to 15-ounce / 397- to 425-g) cans refried beans (nonfat are fine here)
- 2 cups finely shredded mild Cheddar cheese, or 1 cup each finely shredded Monterey Jack and sharp Cheddar cheese
- 2 tablespoons finely chopped fresh cilantro
- Tortilla chips for serving

1. Spray the insert of a 1½ - to 3-quart crock pot with nonstick cooking spray. Cook the sausage in a medium skillet over high heat until it is no longer pink, breaking up any large pieces with the side of a spoon. Drain the sausage and put it in a mixing bowl to cool. Add the onion, chiles, and bell pepper to the same skillet and sauté until the bell pepper is softened, about 5 minutes. Add to the bowl with the sausage and allow to cool slightly. Add the refried beans to the bowl and stir to blend. 2. Spoon half the bean mixture into the slow-cooker insert and sprinkle with half the cheese. Top with the remaining beans and cheese and sprinkle with the cilantro. Cover and cook on low for 2 to 3 hours. 3. Serve from the cooker set at warm and accompany with sturdy tortilla chips.

Hot Broccoli Dip

Prep time: 20 minutes | Cook time: 1 hour | Serves 24

- 2 cups fresh or frozen broccoli, chopped
- 4 tablespoons chopped red bell pepper
- 2 (8-ounce / 227-g)
- containers ranch dip
- ½ cup grated Parmesan cheese
- 2 cups shredded Cheddar cheese

1. In your crock pot, combine all the ingredients thoroughly, ensuring everything is well mixed. 2. Set the cooker to low and let it cook for 1 hour. 3. Once done, serve the dish hot and enjoy!

Barbecue Smokies with Ancho Spice

Prep time: 15 minutes | Cook time: 2 to 3 hours | Serves 6 to 8

- 2 (16-ounce / 454-g) packages mini smoked sausages (Hillshire Farms is a reliable brand)
- 2 tablespoons canola or vegetable oil
- 1 medium onion, finely chopped
- 2 teaspoons ancho chile
- powder
- 1½ cups ketchup
- 1 (8-ounce / 227-g) can tomato sauce
- ¼ cup molasses
- 2 tablespoons Worcestershire sauce
- ¼ cup honey

1. Arrange the sausages in the insert of a 1½- to 3-quart crock pot. Heat the oil in a small skillet over medium-high heat. Add the onion and chili powder and sauté until the onion is softened, about 3 minutes. 2. Transfer the contents of the skillet to the slow-cooker insert. Add the ketchup, tomato sauce, molasses, Worcestershire, and honey and stir to blend. Cover and cook over low heat 2 to 3 hours, until the sausages are heated through. 3. Serve the sausages from the cooker set on warm.

Everyone's Favorite Snack Mix

Prep time: 20 minutes | Cook time: 2 hours | Serves 8 to 10

- ½ cup (2 sticks) unsalted butter, melted
- 2 tablespoons Lawry's seasoned salt
- 1 tablespoon garlic salt
- ¼ cup Worcestershire sauce
- 6 shakes Tabasco sauce
- 4 cups Crispix cereal
- 2 cups mixed nuts
- 1 (8- to 10-ounce / 227- to 283-g) bag pretzel sticks
- 1 (5-ounce / 142-g) bag plain or Parmesan goldfish crackers
- 2 (3-ounce / 85-g) bags herbed croutons

1. In the insert of a 5- to 7-quart crock pot, combine the butter, seasoned salt, garlic salt, Worcestershire sauce, and Tabasco, stirring until the mixture is well blended. Add the remaining ingredients and gently mix to ensure each piece is coated with the flavored butter. 2. Cook the mixture uncovered on high for 2 hours, stirring occasionally to promote even cooking. After 2 hours, reduce the heat to low and continue cooking for another hour, stirring every 15 minutes, until the mixture becomes dry and crisp. 3. Once done, transfer the mixture to baking sheets and allow it to cool completely before serving, or store it in airtight containers for later use.

Tangy Grape-Glazed Meatballs

Prep time: 10 minutes | Cook time: 2 to 4 hours | Serves 15 to 20

- 1 (12-ounce / 340-g) jar grape jelly
- 1 (12-ounce / 340-g) jar chili sauce
- 2 (1-pound / 454-g) bags prepared frozen meatballs, thawed

1. Combine jelly and sauce in crock pot. Stir well. 2. Add meatballs. Stir to coat. 3. Cover and heat on low 4 hours, or on high 2 hours. Keep crock pot on low while serving.

Loaded Veggie Dip

Prep time: 1 hour | Cook time: 1 hour | Makes 5 cups

- ¾ cup finely chopped fresh broccoli
- ½ cup finely chopped cauliflower
- ½ cup finely chopped fresh carrot
- ½ cup finely chopped red onion
- ½ cup finely chopped celery
- 2 garlic cloves, minced
- 4 tablespoons olive oil, divided
- 1 (14-ounce / 397-g) can water-packed artichoke hearts, rinsed, drained and chopped
- 1 (6½-ounce / 184-g) package spreadable garlic
- and herb cream cheese
- 1 (1.4-ounce / 40-g) package vegetable recipe mix (Knorr)
- 1 teaspoon garlic powder
- ½ teaspoon white pepper
- ⅛ to ¼ teaspoon cayenne pepper
- ¼ cup vegetable broth
- ¼ cup half-and-half cream
- 3 cups shredded Italian cheese blend
- ½ cup minced fresh basil
- 1 (9-ounce / 255-g) package fresh spinach, finely chopped
- Assorted crackers or baked pita chips

1. In a large skillet, heat 2 tablespoons of oil and sauté the broccoli, cauliflower, carrot, onion, celery, and garlic until the vegetables are tender. Stir in the artichokes, cream cheese, vegetable recipe mix, garlic powder, white pepper, and cayenne. Set the mixture aside to cool slightly. 2. In a 3-quart crock pot, combine the broth, cream, and remaining oil. Stir in the sautéed vegetable mixture along with the Italian cheese blend and basil. Gently fold in the spinach until well incorporated. 3. Cover the crock pot and cook on low for 1 to 2 hours, or until the cheese has melted and the spinach is tender. 4. Serve the dish hot with crackers on the side for dipping. Enjoy!

Creamy Buffalo Chicken Dip

Prep time: 20 minutes | Cook time: 2 hours | Makes 6 cups

- 2 (8-ounce / 227-g) packages cream cheese, softened
- ½ cup ranch salad dressing
- ½ cup sour cream
- 5 tablespoons crumbled blue cheese
- 2 cups shredded cooked chicken
- ½ cup Buffalo wing sauce
- 2 cups shredded cheddar cheese, divided
- 1 green onion, sliced
- Tortilla chips

1. In a small bowl, combine the cream cheese, dressing, sour cream and blue cheese. Transfer to a 3-quart crock pot. Layer with chicken, wing sauce and 1 cup cheese. Cover and cook on low for 2 to 3 hours or until heated through. 2. Sprinkle with remaining cheese and onion. Serve with tortilla chips.

Zesty Spicy Nut Medley

Prep time: 15 minutes | Cook time: 2 to 2½ hours | Serves 8

- 4 tablespoons (½ stick) unsalted butter, melted
- 2 teaspoons Lawry's seasoned salt
- 1 teaspoon garlic salt
- ⅛ teaspoon cayenne pepper
- 4 tablespoons sugar
- 4 cups pecan halves, walnut halves, or whole almonds

1. Combine the butter, seasoned salt, garlic salt, cayenne, and 2 tablespoons of the sugar in the insert of a 5- to 7-quart crock pot. Cover and cook on high for 20 minutes. 2. Add the nuts and stir to coat with the butter mixture. Cook uncovered for 2 to 2½ hours, stirring occasionally. 3. Sprinkle the remaining 2 tablespoons sugar over the nuts, toss to coat, and remove the nuts to a baking sheet to cool completely before serving.

Tangy Cocktail Franks

Prep time: 10 minutes | Cook time: 1 to 2 hours | Serves 12

- 1 (14-ounce / 397-g) jar currant jelly
- ¼ cup prepared mustard
- 3 tablespoons dry sherry
- ¼ teaspoon ground allspice
- 1 (30-ounce / 850-g) can unsweetened pineapple chunks
- 1 (6-ounce / 170-g) package low-sodium cocktail franks

1. In the crock pot set to high, melt the jelly, stirring until it is fully liquefied and well combined with the seasonings. 2. Drain the pineapple chunks and any liquid from the cocktail franks package, discarding the juice. Gently fold the pineapple and franks into the melted jelly mixture in the crock pot. 3. Cover the crock pot and cook on low for 1 to 2 hours, allowing the flavors to meld. 4. Once ready, serve the dish hot and enjoy!

Ultimate Spinach and Artichoke Dip with Bacon

Prep time: 15 minutes | Cook time: 2 to 3 hours | Serves 8

- 6 strips bacon, cut into ½-inch pieces
- 1 medium onion, finely chopped
- 1 (16-ounce / 454-g) package frozen chopped spinach, defrosted and drained thoroughly
- 1 (16-ounce / 454-g) package frozen artichoke hearts, defrosted, drained, and coarsely chopped, or 2 (14- to 15-ounce / 397- to 425-g) cans artichoke hearts, drained and coarsely chopped
- ¼ teaspoon freshly ground black pepper
- 1½ cups mayonnaise
- 2 cups shredded sharp white Cheddar cheese

1. Cook the bacon in a large skillet until crisp and remove it to paper towels to drain. Remove all but 2 tablespoons of the bacon drippings from the pan and heat over medium-high heat. 2. Add the onion and sauté until it begins to sof ten, about 2 minutes. Add the spinach and artichoke hearts and sauté until the water in the pan has evaporated. Season the mixture with the pepper and turn it out into the insert of a 1½- to 3-quart crock pot. Add the mayonnaise and cheese to the cooker and stir until blended. Cover and cook on low for 2 to 3 hours. 3. Garnish the dip with the bacon bits and serve from the cooker set on warm.

Mini Hot Dogs and Meatballs

Prep time: 5 minutes | Cook time: 2 to 3 hours | Serves 15

- 36 frozen cooked Italian meatballs (½-ounce / 14-g each)
- 1 (16-ounce / 454-g) package miniature hot dogs or little smoked sausages
- 1 (26-ounce / 737-g) jar meatless spaghetti sauce
- 1 (18-ounce / 510-g) bottle barbecue sauce
- 1 (12-ounce / 340-g) bottle chili sauce

1. In the crock pot, add all the ingredients and mix thoroughly to ensure they are well combined. 2. Secure the lid and set the cooker to high for 2 hours or low for 3 hours, allowing the mixture to heat through completely. Serve warm and enjoy your delicious dish!

Decadent Crock Pot Chocolate Clusters

- 1½ pounds (680 g) almond bark, broken
- 1 (4-ounce / 113-g) Baker's Brand German sweet chocolate bar, broken
- 8 ounces (227 g) chocolate chips
- 8 ounces (227 g) peanut butter chips
- 2 pounds (907 g) lightly salted or unsalted peanuts

1. Spray inside of cooker with nonstick cooking spray. 2. Layer ingredients into crock pot in the order given above. 3. Cook on low 2 hours. Do not stir or lift the lid during the cooking time. 4. After 2 hours, mix well. 5. Drop by teaspoonfuls onto waxed paper. Refrigerate for approximately 45 minutes before serving or storing.

Hot Bloody Mary Dip for Shrimp

Prep time: 15 minutes | Cook time: 3 to 4 hours | Serves 8

- 2 (8-ounce / 227-g) packages cream cheese at room temperature, cut into cubes
- 1½ cups Clamato juice
- 2 cups spicy tomato juice or bloody Mary mix
- 2 tablespoons prepared horseradish
- ⅓ cup Worcestershire sauce
- 1 teaspoon Tabasco sauce
- 2 teaspoons celery salt
- ¼ teaspoon freshly ground black pepper
- 2 tablespoons fresh lemon juice
- 1 cup pepper vodka
- 4 green onions, finely chopped, using the white and tender green parts
- 4 stalks celery, finely chopped

1. Lightly coat the insert of a 3- to 5-quart crock pot with nonstick cooking spray. Place the cream cheese in the insert, cover, and cook on low for about 20 minutes, or until it starts to melt. After that, add the remaining ingredients and stir until well combined. 2. Cover the crock pot again and cook on low for 3 to 4 hours, stirring occasionally during the cooking process to ensure even mixing. 3. Once ready, serve the dish directly from the crock pot, keeping it set on warm for serving. Enjoy your meal!

Pizza Dip

Prep time: 15 minutes | Cook time: 3 to 4 hours | Serves 8

- 2 tablespoons extra-virgin olive oil
- 1 medium onion, finely chopped
- 2 teaspoons dried oregano
- 2 teaspoons dried basil
- Pinch of red pepper flakes
- 3 cloves garlic, minced
- 2 (14- to 15-ounce / 397- to 425-g) cans crushed plum tomatoes, with their juice
- 2 tablespoons tomato paste
- 1 ½ teaspoons salt
- ½ teaspoon freshly ground black pepper
- ½ cup finely chopped fresh Italian parsley

1. In a small saucepan, heat the oil over medium-high heat. Add the onion, oregano, basil, red pepper flakes, and garlic, sautéing for about 3 minutes until the onion is softened. 2. Transfer the sautéed mixture to the insert of a 1½- to 3-quart crock pot. Add all the remaining ingredients and stir well to combine. 3. Cover the crock pot and cook on low for 3 to 4 hours, allowing the flavors to meld together. 4. Serve the dish directly from the crock pot, keeping it set on warm to maintain temperature. Enjoy!

Savory BBQ Smoky Bites

Prep time: 5 minutes | Cook time: 4 hours | Serves 48 to 60 as an appetizer

♦ 4 (16-ounce / 454-g) packages little smokies

♦ 1 (18-ounce / 510-g) bottle barbecue sauce

1. Mix ingredients together in crock pot. 2. Cover and cook on low for 4 hours.

Butterscotch Haystacks

Prep time: 15 minutes | Cook time: 15 minutes | Makes 3 dozen pieces

♦ 2 (6-ounce / 170-g) packages butterscotch chips

♦ ¾ cup chopped almonds

♦ 1 (5-ounce / 142-g) can chow mein noodles

1. Set the crock pot to high heat and add the chips. Stir every few minutes until the chips are completely melted and smooth.2. Once melted, gently fold in the almonds and noodles, mixing until everything is well combined.3. Using a teaspoon, drop spoonfuls of the mixture onto waxed paper, forming little haystack shapes.4. Allow the haystacks to sit at room temperature until they are set. For a quicker method, place them in the refrigerator to speed up the setting process.5. Once set, serve the haystacks immediately, or store them in a covered container with waxed paper between layers to keep them from sticking. Store in a cool, dry place for freshness. Enjoy!

Savory Beef Cheese Fondue

Prep time: 20 minutes | Cook time: 6 hours | Makes 2½ cups

♦ 1¾ cups milk

♦ 2 (8-ounce / 227-g) packages cream cheese, cubed

♦ 2 teaspoons dry mustard

♦ ¼ cup chopped green onions

♦ 2½ ounces (71 g) sliced dried beef, shredded or torn into small pieces

♦ French bread, cut into bite-sized pieces, each having a side of crust

1. Heat milk in crock pot on high. 2. Add cheese. Stir until melted. 3. Add mustard, green onions, and dried beef. Stir well. 4. Cover. Cook on low for up to 6 hours. 5. Serve by dipping bread pieces on long forks into mixture.

Chapter **8**

Vegetables and Sides

Chapter 8 Vegetables and Sides

Cheesy Black Bean & Potato Bake

Prep time: 25 minutes | Cook time: 8 hours | Serves 6

- 2 (15-ounce / 425-g) cans black beans, rinsed and drained
- 1 (10¾-ounce / 305-g) can condensed cream of mushroom soup, undiluted
- 1 medium sweet red pepper, chopped
- 1 cup frozen peas
- 1 cup chopped sweet onion
- 1 celery rib, thinly sliced
- 2 garlic cloves, minced
- 1 teaspoon dried thyme
- ¼ teaspoon coarsely ground pepper
- 1½ pounds (680 g) medium red potatoes, cut into ¼-inch slices
- 1 teaspoon salt
- 1 cup shredded cheddar cheese

1. In a large bowl, combine the beans, soup, red pepper, peas, onion, celery, garlic, thyme and pepper. Spoon half of mixture into a greased 3- or 4-quart crock pot. Layer with half of the potatoes, salt and cheese. Repeat layers. Cover and cook on low for 8 to 10 hours or until potatoes are tender.

Barley-Stuffed Cabbage Rolls with Pine Nuts and Currants

Prep time: 20 minutes | Cook time: 6 to 8 hours | Serves 4

- 1 large head green cabbage, cored
- 1 tablespoon olive oil
- 1 large yellow onion, chopped
- 3 cups cooked pearl barley
- 3 ounces (85 g) feta cheese, crumbled
- ½ cup dried currants
- 2 tablespoons pine nuts, toasted
- 2 tablespoons chopped fresh flat-leaf parsley
- ½ teaspoon sea salt
- ½ teaspoon black pepper
- ½ cup apple juice
- 1 tablespoon apple cider vinegar
- 1 (15-ounce / 425-g) can crushed tomatoes, with the juice

1. Steam the entire cabbage head in a large pot over boiling water for 8 minutes. Once done, transfer it to a cutting board and allow it to cool slightly. 2. Carefully remove 16 leaves from the cabbage head, setting aside the remaining cabbage for another recipe. Trim the thick part of the center vein from each leaf, ensuring not to cut out the vein itself. 3. In a large nonstick skillet with a lid, heat the oil over medium heat. Add the chopped onion, cover, and cook for about 6 minutes until it becomes tender. Once cooked, transfer the onion to a large mixing bowl. 4. Into the bowl, stir in the barley, feta cheese, currants, pine nuts, and parsley. Season the mixture with ¼ teaspoon of salt and ¼ teaspoon of pepper, mixing well. 5. Lay the cabbage leaves flat on a clean surface. For each leaf, place about ⅓ cup of the barley mixture in the center. Fold the edges over the filling and roll the leaf up tightly, similar to making a burrito. Repeat this process for the remaining 15 cabbage leaves. 6. Arrange the prepared cabbage rolls in the crock pot in a single layer. 7. In a separate bowl, combine the remaining ¼ teaspoon salt, ¼ teaspoon pepper, apple juice, apple cider vinegar, and tomatoes. Pour this apple juice mixture evenly over the cabbage rolls in the crock pot. 8. Cover the crock pot and cook on high for 2 hours or on low for 6 to 8 hours. Serve the rolls hot and enjoy!

Savory Five-Spice Sweet Potato Medley

Prep time: 15 minutes | Cook time: 5½ to 6 hours | Serves 6 to 8

- 4 large sweet potatoes, peeled, cut into ½-inch-thick slices
- 4 tablespoons (½ stick) unsalted butter, melted and cooled slightly
- 2 tablespoons vegetable oil
- 2 tablespoons soy sauce
- 2 tablespoons rice wine (mirin) or dry sherry
- 2 tablespoons light brown sugar
- 1 teaspoon five-spice powder

1. Coat the insert of a 5- to 7-quart crock pot with nonstick cooking spray or line it with a slow-cooker liner according to the manufacturer's directions. 2. Arrange the sweet potatoes in the slow-cooker insert. Combine the remaining ingredients in a mixing bowl and pour over the potatoes in the slow-cooker insert. 3. Cover and cook on low for 5½ to 6 hours, until the sweet potatoes are tender when pierced with the tip of a paring knife. 4. Serve the sweet potatoes from the cooker set on warm.

Simply Sweet Potatoes

Prep time: 5 minutes | Cook time: 6 to 9 hours | Serves 4

- 3 large sweet potatoes
- ¼ cup water

1. Begin by placing the unpeeled sweet potatoes directly into the crock pot. 2. Pour in ¼ cup of water to help with steaming. 3. Cover the pot and set it to high for 1 hour. After that, switch to low and cook for an additional 5 to 8 hours, or until the sweet potatoes are fork-tender. Enjoy your perfectly cooked sweet potatoes!

Creamy Corn Casserole Delight

Prep time: 10 minutes | Cook time: 3 to 6 hours | Serves 6

- 2 eggs
- 1 (10¾-ounce / 305-g) can cream of celery soup
- ⅔ cup unseasoned bread crumbs
- 2 cups whole-kernel corn, drained, or cream-style corn
- 1 teaspoon minced onion
- ¼ to ½ teaspoon salt, according to your taste preference
- ⅛ teaspoon pepper
- 1 tablespoon sugar
- 2 tablespoons butter, melted

1. Beat eggs with fork. Add soup and bread crumbs. Mix well. 2. Add remaining ingredients and mix thoroughly. Pour into greased crock pot. 3. Cover. Cook on high 3 hours, or on low 6 hours.

Cheesy Pizzaiola Potatoes

Prep time: 30 minutes | Cook time: 5 to 8 hours | Serves 6 to 8

- 4 tablespoons extra-virgin olive oil
- 2 cloves garlic, minced
- 2 teaspoons dried oregano
- 1 (28- to 32-ounce / 794- to 907-g) can crushed tomatoes
- 2½ teaspoons salt
- 1 teaspoon freshly ground black pepper
- 8 medium red potatoes, scrubbed and cut into ¼-inch-thick slices
- ½ medium red onion, cut into thin half rounds (about ¼ cup)
- 2 cups shredded Mozzarella
- 1 cup freshly grated Parmigiano-Reggiano cheese

1. Coat the insert of a 5- to 7-quart crock pot with nonstick cooking spray or line it with a slow-cooker liner according to the manufacturer's directions. 2. heat 2 tablespoons of the oil in a large saucepan over medium-high heat. Add the garlic and oregano and sauté for 30 seconds, until fragrant. 3. Add the tomatoes, 1 teaspoon of the salt, and ½ teaspoon of the pepper and stir to combine.

Simmer uncovered for 30 to 45 minutes. Taste and adjust the seasoning. Put the potatoes, onion, remaining 1½ teaspoons salt, ½ teaspoon pepper, and 2 tablespoons oil in a large mixing bowl and toss until the potatoes and onion are coated. In another bowl, mix together the cheeses. 4. Pour ½ to ¾ cup of the sauce to cover the bottom of the slow-cooker insert. Top with half the potatoes and sprinkle with half the cheese. Spoon an even layer of sauce over the top. Repeat the layers with the remaining potatoes, cheese, and sauce. Cover and cook on high for 5 hours or on low for 8 hours. 5. Serve from the cooker set on warm.

Zesty Swiss-Irish Tomato Sauce

Prep time: 15 minutes | Cook time: 4 hours | Serves 6 to 8

- 2 medium onions, diced
- 5 garlic cloves, minced
- ¼ cup oil
- 1 (1-pound / 454-g) can tomatoes, puréed
- 1 (15-ounce / 425-g) can tomato sauce
- 1 (12-ounce / 340-g) can tomato paste
- 2 tablespoons parsley, fresh
- or dried
- ½ teaspoon red pepper
- ½ teaspoon black pepper
- 1 teaspoon chili powder
- 1 teaspoon dried basil
- 2 teaspoons Worcestershire sauce
- 2 teaspoons Tabasco sauce
- ¼ cup red wine

1. Sauté onions and garlic in oil in skillet. 2. Combine all ingredients in crock pot. 3. Cover. Cook on low 4 hours. 4. Serve.

Pizza Potatoes

Prep time: 15 minutes | Cook time: 6 to 10 hours | Serves 4 to 6

- 6 medium potatoes, sliced
- 1 large onion, thinly sliced
- 2 tablespoons olive oil
- 2 cups shredded Mozzarella cheese
- 2 ounces (57 g) sliced pepperoni
- 1 teaspoon salt
- 1 (8-ounce / 227-g) can pizza sauce

1. In a skillet, sauté the potato and onion slices in oil over medium heat until the onions become transparent. Once cooked, drain the mixture well to remove excess oil. 2. In the crock pot, combine the sautéed potatoes and onions with cheese, pepperoni, and salt, stirring to mix everything evenly. 3. Pour the pizza sauce over the top of the mixture, ensuring it covers the ingredients well. 4. Cover the crock pot and cook on low for 6 to 10 hours, or until the potatoes are tender and soft. Serve hot and enjoy!

Caponata

Prep time: 25 minutes | Cook time: 6 hours |
Serves 6

- 2 tablespoons extra-virgin olive oil
- 1 medium red onion, finely chopped
- 3 cloves garlic, minced
- 3 stalks celery, finely chopped
- 2 medium purple eggplants, finely diced
- 2 medium red bell peppers, seeded and cut into ½-inch pieces
- 1 teaspoon dried oregano
- 1 teaspoon salt
- Pinch of red pepper flakes
- ¼ cup balsamic vinegar
- 1 (15-ounce / 425-g) can diced tomatoes, with their juice
- 1 cup golden raisins
- ¼ cup brined capers, drained
- ½ cup pitted Kalamata olives (or your favorite olive)
- ½ cup finely chopped fresh Italian parsley

1. In a large skillet, heat the oil over medium-high heat. Add the onion, garlic, and celery, sautéing until the onion is softened, which should take about 3 minutes. 2. Once cooked, transfer the mixture from the skillet to the insert of a 5- to 7-quart crock pot. In the same skillet, add the eggplants, bell peppers, oregano, salt, and red pepper flakes, sautéing until the eggplant starts to soften, about 4 to 5 minutes. Add the vinegar and let it cook off slightly, then stir in the tomatoes and raisins. 3. Transfer the contents of the skillet to the crock pot and stir everything together until well combined. Cover the crock pot and cook on low for 5 hours. After this time, stir in the capers, olives, and parsley, then cook for an additional hour, until the eggplant is tender. 4. Once done, remove the caponata from the crock pot and serve it either cold or at room temperature for the best flavor.

Zucchini in Sour Cream

Prep time: 10 minutes | Cook time: 1 to 1½
hours | Serves 6

- 4 cups unpeeled, sliced zucchini
- 1 cup fat-free sour cream
- ¼ cup skim milk
- 1 cup chopped onions
- 1 teaspoon salt
- 1 cup shredded low-fat sharp Cheddar cheese
- Nonfat cooking spray

1. Begin by parboiling the zucchini in the microwave for 2 to 3 minutes to soften slightly. Transfer the zucchini to a crock pot that has been sprayed with nonfat cooking spray. 2. In a separate bowl, mix together the sour cream, milk, onions, and salt until well combined. Pour this mixture over the zucchini and stir gently to coat the zucchini evenly. 3. Cover the crock pot and set it to cook on low for 1 to 1½ hours, allowing the flavors to meld. 4. About 30 minutes before serving, sprinkle cheese over the top of the vegetables to melt. Enjoy your creamy zucchini dish!

Bacon-Tomato Green Bean Medley

Prep time: 15 minutes | Cook time: 4½ hours |
Serves 12

- 1 (14-ounce / 397-g) package thick-sliced bacon strips, chopped
- 1 large red onion, chopped
- 2 (16-ounce / 454-g) packages frozen cut green beans
- 1 (28-ounce / 794-g) can
- petite diced tomatoes, undrained
- ¼ cup packed brown sugar
- 1 tablespoon seasoned pepper
- ½ teaspoon seasoned salt
- 1 (16-ounce / 454-g) can red beans, rinsed and drained

1. In a large skillet, cook bacon over medium heat until partially cooked but not crisp, stirring occasionally. Remove with a slotted spoon; drain on paper towels. Discard drippings, reserving 2 tablespoons. Add onion to drippings; cook and stir over medium-high heat until tender. 2. In a 4- or 5-quart crock pot, combine green beans, tomatoes, brown sugar, pepper, salt, bacon and onion. Cook, covered, on low 4 hours. Stir in red beans. Cook 30 minutes longer or until heated through.

Herb-Infused Sourdough Stuffing

Prep time: 25 minutes | Cook time: 4 to 5 hours
| Serves 8

- 3 tablespoons butter
- 3 onions, chopped
- 4 celery ribs, chopped
- ½ cup chopped fresh parsley
- 1 tablespoon chopped fresh rosemary
- 1 tablespoon chopped fresh thyme
- 1 tablespoon chopped fresh marjoram
- 1 tablespoon chopped fresh sage
- 1 teaspoon salt
- ½ teaspoon freshly-ground black pepper
- 1 loaf stale low-fat sourdough bread, cut in 1-inch cubes
- 2 cups fat-free chicken broth

1. Sauté onions and celery in butter in skillet until transparent. Remove from heat and stir in fresh herbs and seasonings. 2. Place bread cubes in large bowl. Add onion/herb mixture. Add enough broth to moisten. Mix well but gently. Turn into greased crock pot. 3. Cover. Cook on high 1 hour. Reduce heat to low and continue cooking 3 to 4 hours.

Spicy Creamer Potatoes

- 2 pounds (907 g) creamer potatoes
- 1 onion, chopped
- 3 garlic cloves, minced
- 1 chipotle chile in adobo sauce, minced
- 2 tablespoons freshly

- squeezed lemon juice
- 2 tablespoons water
- 1 tablespoon chili powder
- ½ teaspoon ground cumin
- ½ teaspoon salt
- ⅛ teaspoon freshly ground black pepper

1. Add all the ingredients to the crock pot and mix well to ensure everything is combined. 2. Cover the pot and set it to cook on low for 7 to 8 hours, or until the potatoes are tender. Once done, serve hot and enjoy your dish!

Sweet and Spicy Creole Green Beans

- 2 small onions, chopped
- Half a stick butter
- 4 cups green beans, fresh or frozen

- ½ cup salsa
- 2 to 3 tablespoons brown sugar
- ½ teaspoon garlic salt (optional)

1. Sauté onions in butter in a saucepan. 2. Combine with remaining ingredients in crock pot. 3. Cover and cook on low 3 to 4 hours, or longer, depending upon how soft or crunchy you like your beans.

Broccoli Delight

- 1 to 2 pounds (454 to 907 g) broccoli, chopped
- 2 cups cauliflower, chopped
- 1 (10¾-ounce / 305-g) can 98% fat-free cream of celery soup
- ½ teaspoon salt

- ¼ teaspoon black pepper
- 1 medium onion, diced
- 2 to 4 garlic cloves, crushed, according to your taste preference
- ½ cup vegetable broth

1. In the crock pot, mix all the ingredients together until well combined. 2. Set the cooker to low and cook for 4 to 6 hours, or on high for 2 to 3 hours, allowing the flavors to meld and the dish to cook thoroughly. Serve hot and enjoy!

Squash Casserole

- 2 pounds (907 g) yellow summer squash or zucchini thinly sliced (about 6 cups)
- Half a medium onion, chopped
- 1 cup peeled, shredded carrot
- 1 (10¾-ounce / 305-g) can

- condensed cream of chicken soup
- 1 cup sour cream
- ¼ cup flour
- 1 (8-ounce / 227-g) package seasoned stuffing crumbs
- ½ cup butter, melted

1. In a large bowl, combine the squash, onion, carrots, and soup, mixing well to combine all ingredients. 2. In a separate bowl, mix the sour cream and flour until smooth, then stir this mixture into the vegetables until fully incorporated. 3. In another bowl, toss the stuffing crumbs with melted butter, then spread half of the crumbs evenly in the bottom of the crock pot. Pour the vegetable mixture over the crumbs and top with the remaining crumbs. 4. Cover the crock pot and cook on low for 7 to 9 hours, allowing the flavors to meld together. Enjoy your delicious dish!

Cheesy Bacon Mash Delight

- 8 large russet potatoes, peeled and cut into 1-inch chunks
- 4 tablespoons (½ stick) unsalted butter
- 1 cup finely shredded mild Cheddar cheese
- 1 (8-ounce / 227-g) package cream cheese at room

- temperature
- 1 cup sour cream
- 4 green onions, finely chopped, using the white and tender green parts
- 8 strips bacon, cooked crisp, drained, and crumbled
- Salt and freshly ground black pepper

1. Coat the insert of a 5- to 7-quart crock pot with nonstick cooking spray or line with a slow-cooker liner according to the manufacturer's directions. 2. Cook the potatoes in salted water to cover until tender when pierced with the tip of a sharp knife. Drain the potatoes thoroughly and place in the bowl of an electric mixer. 3. Add 2 tablespoons of the butter, ½ cup of the Cheddar, the cream cheese, and sour cream and beat until fluffy and light. Stir in the green onions and bacon and season with salt and pepper. Transfer the potato mixture to the slow-cooker insert and top with the remaining butter and cheese. 4. Cover and cook on low for 3 to 4 hours, until the butter is melted and the potatoes are heated through. 5. Serve the potatoes from the cooker set on warm.

Mjeddrah

- 10 cups water
- 4 cups dried lentils, rinsed
- 2 cups brown rice, uncooked
- ¼ cup olive oil
- 2 teaspoons salt

1. In a large crock pot, mix all the ingredients together thoroughly until well combined. 2. Cover the pot and set it to cook on high for 8 hours, then reduce the heat to low and continue cooking for an additional 2 hours. If necessary, add 2 more cups of water during cooking to ensure the rice cooks properly and to prevent the dish from drying out. 3. Once cooked, serve hot and enjoy your meal!

Sweet and Savory Tzimmes Stew

- 1 to 2 sweet potatoes
- 6 carrots, sliced
- 1 potato, peeled and diced
- 1 onion, chopped
- 2 apples, peeled and sliced
- 1 butternut squash, peeled and sliced
- ¼ cup dry white wine or apple juice
- ½ pound (227 g) dried apricots
- 1 tablespoon ground cinnamon
- 1 tablespoon apple pie spice
- 1 tablespoon maple syrup or honey
- 1 teaspoon salt
- 1 teaspoon ground ginger

1. Combine all ingredients in large crock pot, or mix all ingredients in large bowl and then divide between 2 (4- to 5-quart) cookers. 2. Cover. Cook on low 10 hours.

Pineapple Sweet Potatoes

- 1 (10-ounce / 283-g) can unsweetened crushed pineapple, drained
- 2 tablespoons dark brown sugar
- 1 (40-ounce / 1.1-kg) can unsweetened yams, drained
- Cooking spray

1. In a bowl, mix the crushed pineapples with the brown sugar until well combined. 2. Transfer the pineapple mixture to a crock pot that has been sprayed with cooking spray, then add the yams and stir to combine. 3. Cover the crock pot and cook on low for 2 to 4 hours, or until everything is heated through. Enjoy your dish!

Cinnamon-Apple Sweet Potatoes

- 2 pounds (907 g) sweet potatoes or yams
- 1½ cups applesauce
- ⅔ cup brown sugar
- 3 tablespoons butter, melted
- 1 teaspoon cinnamon
- Chopped nuts (optional)

1. Peel sweet potatoes if you wish. Cut into cubes or slices. Place in crock pot. 2. In a bowl, mix together applesauce, brown sugar, butter, and cinnamon. Spoon over potatoes. 3. Cover and cook on low 6 to 8 hours, or until potatoes are tender. 4. Mash potatoes and sauce together if you wish with a large spoon—or spoon potatoes into serving dish and top with the sauce. 5. Sprinkle with nuts, if you want.

Apricot-Chestnut Stuffing

- Nonstick cooking spray
- 3 tablespoons butter
- 1 onion, chopped
- 1 leek, white part only, chopped
- 3 garlic cloves, minced
- 1 (16 ounces / 454 g) can whole peeled chestnuts, chopped
- ⅔ cup chopped dried apricots
- ½ cup chopped walnuts
- 8 slices whole-wheat bread, cut into 1-inch cubes
- 2 eggs, beaten
- ¼ cup milk
- ¼ cup vegetable broth
- 1 teaspoon salt
- ½ teaspoon dried thyme leaves
- ½ teaspoon dried basil leaves
- ⅛ teaspoon freshly ground black pepper

1. Start by spraying the insert of the crock pot with nonstick cooking spray to prevent sticking. 2. In a medium saucepan over medium heat, melt the butter. Once melted, add the onion, leek, and garlic, sautéing and stirring until they become tender, about 5 minutes. Transfer this mixture to the crock pot. 3. Next, add the chestnuts, apricots, walnuts, and bread to the crock pot, mixing well to combine. 4. In a separate small bowl, whisk together the eggs, milk, broth, salt, thyme, basil, and pepper until smooth. Pour this egg mixture into the crock pot and stir to evenly coat all the ingredients. 5. Cover the crock pot and cook on low for 7 to 8 hours, or until the stuffing reaches an internal temperature of 165°F (74°C) as measured with a food thermometer. Once done, serve hot and enjoy!

Golden Carrots

Prep time: 5 minutes | Cook time: 3 to 4 hours | Serves 6

- 1 (2-pound / 907-g) package baby carrots
- ½ cup golden raisins
- 1 stick butter, melted or softened
- ⅓ cup honey
- 2 tablespoons lemon juice
- ½ teaspoon ground ginger (optional)

1. In the crock pot, add all the ingredients and mix them well to combine. 2. Cover the pot and set it to cook on low for 3 to 4 hours, or until the carrots are tender-crisp. Serve warm and enjoy!

Herbed Coconut Pumpkin Mash

Prep time: 15 minutes | Cook time: 7 to 8 hours | Serves 6

- 3 tablespoons extra-virgin olive oil, divided
- 1 pound (454 g) pumpkin, cut into 1-inch chunks
- ½ cup coconut milk
- 1 tablespoon apple cider
- vinegar
- ½ teaspoon chopped thyme
- 1 teaspoon chopped oregano
- ¼ teaspoon salt
- 1 cup Greek yogurt

1. Lightly grease the insert of the crock pot with 1 tablespoon of the olive oil. 2. Add the remaining 2 tablespoons of the olive oil with the pumpkin, coconut milk, apple cider vinegar, thyme, oregano, and salt to the insert. 3. Cover and cook on low for 7 to 8 hours. 4. Mash the pumpkin with the yogurt using a potato masher until smooth. 5. Serve warm.

Cheesy Onions

Prep time: 20 minutes | Cook time: 2 to 4 hours | Serves 6 to 8

- 1½ pounds (680 g) small onions
- 4 slices bacon, cooked and crumbled
- 1 (10½-ounce / 298-g) can
- Cheddar cheese soup
- ½ cup milk
- ¼ cup grated Parmesan cheese

1. Peel the onions, keeping them whole, and place them in the crock pot. 2. In a separate bowl, combine all the remaining ingredients thoroughly. 3. Pour this mixture into the crock pot and gently mix it with the onions to coat them evenly. 4. Cover the pot and cook on high for 2 hours or on low for 4 hours, until the onions are completely tender. Enjoy your dish!

Cheesy Hash Browns

Prep time: 10 minutes | Cook time: 7 hours | Serves ¾ cup

- Nonstick cooking spray
- 1 (20 ounces / 567 g) package frozen hash brown potatoes
- 1 onion, finely chopped
- 3 garlic cloves, minced
- 1 cup grated Colby or Gruyère cheese
- 1 cup milk
- ⅓ cup heavy cream
- 3 tablespoons butter
- ½ teaspoon dried marjoram leaves
- ¼ teaspoon salt
- ⅛ teaspoon freshly ground black pepper
- ½ cup sour cream

1. Begin by spraying the inside of the crock pot with nonstick cooking spray to prevent sticking. 2. In the crock pot, combine the hash brown potatoes, onion, and garlic, stirring until evenly mixed. Add the cheese and mix again to incorporate it. 3. In a small saucepan over high heat, combine the milk, cream, butter, marjoram, salt, and pepper. Heat the mixture until the butter melts, which should take about a minute. Remove from heat and stir in the sour cream until well blended. 4. Pour the creamy milk mixture into the crock pot, ensuring it covers the potato mixture. 5. Cover the crock pot and cook on low for 7 hours, or until the potatoes are tender. Once done, serve hot and enjoy your dish!

Vegetable Curry

Prep time: 15 minutes | Cook time: 3 to 10 hours | Serves 8 to 10

- 1 (16-ounce / 454-g) package baby carrots
- 3 medium potatoes, cubed
- 1 pound (454 g) fresh or frozen green beans, cut in 2-inch pieces
- 1 green pepper, chopped
- 1 onion, chopped
- 1 to 2 cloves garlic, minced
- 1 (15-ounce / 425-g) can garbanzo beans, drained
- 1 (28-ounce / 794-g) can crushed tomatoes
- 3 tablespoons minute tapioca
- 3 teaspoons curry powder
- 2 teaspoons salt
- 1¾ cups boiling water
- 2 teaspoons chicken bouillon granules, or 2 chicken bouillon cubes

1. In a large bowl, mix together the carrots, potatoes, green beans, bell pepper, onion, garlic, garbanzo beans, and crushed tomatoes until well combined. 2. Stir in the tapioca, curry powder, and salt, ensuring everything is evenly distributed. 3. Dissolve the bouillon in a cup of boiling water, then pour it over the vegetable mixture and mix thoroughly. Spoon the mixture into a large crock pot or divide it between two medium-sized ones. 4. Cover the crock pot(s) and cook on low for 8 to 10 hours, or on high for 3 to 4 hours. Once cooked, serve hot and enjoy!

Creamy Cheesy Corn Delight

- 3 (16-ounce / 454-g) packages frozen corn
- 1 (8-ounce / 227-g) package cream cheese, cubed
- ¼ cup butter, cubed
- 3 tablespoons water
- 3 tablespoons milk
- 2 tablespoons sugar
- 6 slices American cheese, cut into squares

1. Combine all ingredients in crock pot. Mix well. 2. Cover. Cook on low 4 hours, or until heated through and the cheese is melted.

Soy-Glazed Green Beans with Cipollini Onions and Cremini Mushrooms

- ½ cup (1 stick) unsalted butter, melted
- ¼ cup soy sauce
- 2 tablespoons rice wine (mirin) or dry sherry
- 2 cloves garlic, minced
- 24 cipollini onions, peeled
- 8 ounces (227 g) cremini mushrooms, quartered
- 2 pounds (907 g) green beans, ends trimmed, cut into 1-inch lengths

1. Combine the butter, soy sauce, rice wine, and garlic into the insert of a 5- to 7-quart crock pot and stir to blend. 2. Add the remaining ingredients and toss to coat with the butter mixture. Cover and cook on low for 4 to 5 hours, until the beans and onions are tender. 3. Drain the liquid from the vegetables and serve the vegetables immediately.

Cheesy Potato Bake with Crunchy Croutons

- 6 potatoes, peeled and cut into ¼-inch strips
- 2 cups sharp Cheddar cheese, shredded
- 1 (10¾-ounce / 305-g) can cream of chicken soup
- 1 small onion, chopped
- 7 tablespoons butter, melted, divided
- 1 teaspoon salt
- 1 teaspoon pepper
- 1 cup sour cream
- 2 cups seasoned stuffing cubes

1. Toss together potatoes and cheese. Place in crock pot. 2.

Combine soup, onion, 4 tablespoons butter, salt, and pepper. Pour over potatoes. 3. Cover. Cook on low 8 hours. 4. Stir in sour cream. Cover and heat for 10 more minutes. 5. Meanwhile, toss together stuffing cubes and 3 tablespoons butter. Sprinkle over potatoes just before serving.

Squash Medley

- 8 summer squash, each about 4-inches long, thinly sliced
- ½ teaspoon salt
- 2 tomatoes, peeled and chopped
- ¼ cup sliced green onions
- Half a small sweet green pepper, chopped
- 1 chicken bouillon cube
- ¼ cup hot water
- 4 slices bacon, fried and crumbled
- ¼ cup fine dry bread crumbs

1. Begin by sprinkling the squash with salt to enhance its flavor. 2. In the crock pot, create layers by adding half of the squash, followed by tomatoes, onions, and bell pepper. Repeat this layering process with the remaining ingredients. 3. Dissolve the bouillon in hot water, then pour the mixture into the crock pot, ensuring it seeps through the layers. 4. Top the layered vegetables with bacon, then sprinkle bread crumbs evenly over the top for added texture. 5. Cover the crock pot and cook on low for 4 to 6 hours, allowing the flavors to meld together beautifully. Enjoy your dish when ready!

Creamed Vegetables

- 1 tablespoon extra-virgin olive oil
- ½ head cauliflower, cut into small florets
- 2 cups green beans, cut into 2-inch pieces
- 1 cup asparagus spears, cut into 2-inch pieces
- ½ cup sour cream
- ½ cup shredded Cheddar cheese
- ½ cup shredded Swiss cheese
- 3 tablespoons butter
- ¼ cup water
- 1 teaspoon ground nutmeg
- Pinch freshly ground black pepper, for seasoning

1. Begin by lightly greasing the insert of the crock pot with olive oil to prevent sticking. 2. Add the cauliflower, green beans, asparagus, sour cream, Cheddar cheese, Swiss cheese, butter, water, nutmeg, and pepper to the insert, mixing everything together well. 3. Cover the crock pot and set it to cook on low for 6 hours, allowing the flavors to meld. 4. Once cooked, serve the dish warm and enjoy!

Garlic-Rosemary Roasted Potatoes

Prep time: 10 minutes | Cook time: 4 hours | Serves 8

- ½ cup extra-virgin olive oil
- 6 cloves garlic, sliced
- 2 teaspoons fresh rosemary leaves, finely chopped
- 2 teaspoons coarse salt
- 1 teaspoon coarsely ground black pepper
- 16 to 20 small (2-inch) red potatoes, scrubbed

1. Combine all the ingredients in the insert of a 5- to 7-quart crock pot cover and cook on high for 4 hours, stirring after 2 hours to bring the potatoes from the bottom to the top. 2. Serve immediately, or keep warm for up to 2 hours in the cooker set on warm.

Southern-Style Green Beans

Prep time: 10 minutes | Cook time: 6 hours | Serves 6 to 8

- 6 strips bacon, cut into 1-inch pieces; reserve some for garnish
- 2 pounds (907 g) green beans, ends snipped, cut into 1-inch pieces
- 1 medium onion, coarsely chopped
- 1½ cups chicken broth
- 4 cloves garlic, peeled
- 6 whole black peppercorns

1. In the insert of a 5- to 7-quart crock pot, mix all the ingredients together thoroughly. Cover the pot and set it to cook on low for 6 hours, or until the beans are tender and flavorful. 2. Once the cooking time is complete, drain the beans and discard any peppercorns and garlic that remain in the pot. 3. Serve the beans hot, garnished with the reserved bacon for added flavor and texture. Enjoy your meal!

Maple-Sage Sweet Potatoes with Apples

Prep time: 15 minutes | Cook time: 6 to 8 hours | Serves 8 to 10

- 3 large sweet potatoes, peeled and cubed
- 3 large tart and firm apples, peeled and sliced
- ½ to ¾ teaspoon salt
- ⅛ to ¼ teaspoon pepper
- 1 teaspoon sage
- 1 teaspoon ground cinnamon
- 4 tablespoons (½ stick) butter, melted
- ¼ cup maple syrup
- Toasted sliced almonds or chopped pecans (optional)

1. Place half the sweet potatoes in crock pot. Layer in half the apple slices. 2. Mix together seasonings. Sprinkle half over apples. 3. Mix together butter and maple syrup. Spoon half over seasonings. 4. Repeat layers. 5. Cover. Cook on low 6 to 8 hours or until potatoes are soft, stirring occasionally. 6. To add a bit of crunch, sprinkle with toasted almonds or pecans when serving. 7. Serve.

Sweet and Savory Braised Red Cabbage

Prep time: 15 minutes | Cook time: 7 to 8 hours | Serves 8

- 1 tablespoon extra-virgin olive oil
- 1 small red cabbage, coarsely shredded (about 6 cups)
- ½ sweet onion, thinly sliced
- ¼ cup apple cider vinegar
- 3 tablespoons granulated erythritol
- 2 teaspoons minced garlic
- ½ teaspoon ground nutmeg
- ⅛ teaspoon ground cloves
- 2 tablespoons butter
- Salt, for seasoning
- Freshly ground black pepper, for seasoning
- ½ cup chopped walnuts, for garnish
- ½ cup crumbled blue cheese, for garnish
- Pink peppercorns, for garnish (optional)

1. Lightly grease the insert of the crock pot with the olive oil. 2. Add the cabbage, onion, apple cider vinegar, erythritol, garlic, nutmeg, and cloves to the insert, stirring to mix well. 3. Break off little slices of butter and scatter them on top of the cabbage mixture. 4. Cover and cook on low for 7 to 8 hours. 5. Season with salt and pepper. 6. Serve topped with the walnuts, blue cheese, and peppercorns (if desired).

Riesling-Infused Caraway Cabbage

Prep time: 10 minutes | Cook time: 4 to 5 hours | Serves 6 to 8

- 2 tablespoons olive oil
- 2 medium sweet onions, finely chopped
- 2 teaspoons caraway seeds
- 10 cups thinly sliced green
- cabbage (about 2 medium heads)
- 2 cups Riesling wine
- 1 teaspoon freshly ground black pepper

1. Heat the oil in a large skillet over medium-high heat. Add the onions and caraway seeds and sauté until the onions are softened, about 3 minutes. Transfer the contents of the skillet to the insert of a 5- to 7-quart crock pot. 2. Add the cabbage, Riesling, and pepper and stir to coat the cabbage and distribute the ingredients. Cover and cook on low for 4 to 5 hours, until the cabbage is tender. 3. Serve from the cooker set on warm.

Creamy Mashed Potatoes

Prep time: 15 minutes | Cook time: 3 to 5 hours | Serves 10 to 12

- 2 teaspoons salt
- 6 tablespoons (¾ stick) butter, melted
- 2¼ cups milk
- 6⅞ cups potato flakes
- 6 cups water
- 1 cup sour cream
- 4 to 5 ounces (113 to 142 g) cream cheese, softened

1. In a mixing bowl, combine the first five ingredients according to the instructions on the potato box, preparing them as directed. 2. Using an electric mixer, whip the cream cheese until it becomes creamy, then blend in the sour cream until fully incorporated. 3. Gently fold the prepared potatoes into the cream cheese and sour cream mixture, beating well to combine everything thoroughly. Transfer the mixture to the crock pot. 4. Cover the crock pot and cook on low for 3 to 5 hours, allowing the flavors to meld and the dish to heat through. Enjoy your delicious potato dish!

Stuffed Mushrooms

Prep time: 20 minutes | Cook time: 2 to 4 hours | Serves 4 to 6

- 8 to 10 large mushrooms
- ¼ teaspoon minced garlic
- 1 tablespoon oil
- Dash of salt
- Dash of pepper
- Dash of cayenne pepper (optional)
- ¼ cup shredded Monterey Jack cheese

1. Begin by removing the stems from the mushrooms and dicing them into small pieces. 2. In a skillet, heat the oil over medium heat. Sauté the diced mushroom stems with garlic until they are softened, then remove the skillet from the heat. 3. Stir in your choice of seasonings and cheese, mixing until well combined. Stuff the mixture into the mushroom caps and place them in the crock pot. 4. Cover the crock pot and heat on low for 2 to 4 hours, allowing the flavors to meld and the mushrooms to cook through. Enjoy your delicious stuffed mushrooms!

Slow-Cooked Sweet Potatoes

Prep time: 5 minutes | Cook time: 6 hours | Serves 6 to 8

- 6 to 8 medium sweet potatoes, scrubbed

1. Prick each potato a few times with the tip of a sharp paring knife. Arrange the potatoes in the insert of a 5- to 7-quart crock pot. Cover and cook on low for 6 hours, until the potatoes are tender when pierced with the tip of a knife. 2. Serve the potatoes split open.

Chapter **9**

Desserts

Chapter 9 Desserts

Down East Indian Pudding

Prep time: 20 minutes | Cook time: 3 hours | Serves 8

- ½ cup yellow cornmeal
- ¾ cup water
- 4 cups milk
- 1 large egg
- 3 tablespoons sugar
- ½ cup dark molasses
- 2 tablespoons unsalted butter
- 1 teaspoon ground

- cinnamon
- 1 teaspoon ground ginger
- ½ teaspoon ground nutmeg
- ¼ teaspoon salt
- ½ cup raisins or other dried fruits, such as cranberries or blueberries
- 2½ cups heavy cream
- ¼ cup maple syrup

1. Begin by spraying the insert of a 5- to 7-quart crock pot with nonstick cooking spray to prevent sticking. In a large mixing bowl, combine all the ingredients except for the heavy cream and maple syrup, stirring until everything is well blended. Transfer this mixture into the slow-cooker insert. 2. Cover the crock pot and cook on high for 3 hours, or until the pudding is set. Once done, carefully remove the slow-cooker insert and let the pudding cool for about 30 minutes. 3. In a mixing bowl, whip the heavy cream until stiff peaks form, then gradually beat in the maple syrup until fully incorporated. 4. Serve the warm pudding directly from the crock pot, accompanied by the maple-flavored whipped cream for a delightful touch. Enjoy your dessert!

Brownies with Nuts

Prep time: 15 minutes | Cook time: 3 hours | Makes 24 brownies

- Half a stick butter, melted
- 1 cup chopped nuts, divided

- 1 (23-ounce / 652-g) package brownie mix

1. Begin by pouring melted butter into a baking insert that fits inside your crock pot, swirling it around to grease the sides of the insert. 2. Sprinkle half of the nuts evenly over the melted butter. 3. In a mixing bowl, prepare the brownie batter according to the package instructions. Spoon half of the batter into the greased baking insert, ensuring it covers the nuts evenly. 4. Add the remaining half of the nuts on top, then spoon in the rest of the brownie batter to cover them. 5. Place the baking insert into the crock pot, and cover it

with 8 paper towels to absorb moisture. 6. Put the lid on the crock pot and cook on high for 3 hours without lifting the lid until the last hour of cooking. After that, insert a toothpick into the center of the brownies. If it comes out clean, they are done; if not, continue cooking for another 15 minutes, then check again, repeating this process until the toothpick comes out clean. 7. Once cooking is complete, carefully uncover the crock pot and the baking insert. Allow the brownies to stand for 5 minutes. 8. Invert the insert onto a serving plate and cut the brownies using a plastic knife to avoid dragging the crumbs. Serve warm and enjoy!

Sour-Cream Cheesecake

Prep time: 10 minutes | Cook time: 5 to 6 hours | Serves 10

- ¼ cup butter, melted, divided
- 1 cup ground almonds
- ¾ cup plus 1 tablespoon granulated erythritol, divided
- ¼ teaspoon ground

- cinnamon
- 12 ounces (340 g) cream cheese, at room temperature
- 2 eggs
- 2 teaspoons pure vanilla extract
- 1 cup sour cream

1. Begin by lightly greasing a 7-inch springform pan with 1 tablespoon of butter to prevent sticking. 2. In a small bowl, mix together the almonds, 1 tablespoon of erythritol, and cinnamon until well combined. 3. Add the remaining 3 tablespoons of butter to the mixture and stir until it forms coarse crumbs. 4. Press this crust mixture firmly into the bottom of the springform pan and up the sides, about 2 inches high. 5. In a large mixing bowl, use a handheld mixer to beat together the cream cheese, eggs, vanilla extract, and the remaining ¾ cup of erythritol until smooth. Fold in the sour cream until fully blended and creamy. 6. Spoon the batter into the prepared springform pan, smoothing the top with a spatula. 7. Place a wire rack in the insert of the crock pot and set the springform pan on top of the rack. 8. Cover the crock pot and cook on low for 5 to 6 hours, or until the cheesecake no longer jiggles when gently shaken. 9. Once cooked, allow the cheesecake to cool completely before removing it from the pan. 10. For the best flavor and texture, chill the cheesecake in the refrigerator completely before serving, and be sure to store any leftovers in the fridge. Enjoy your delicious cheesecake!

Cinnamon-Infused Apple Delight

Prep time: 20 minutes | Cook time: 2 to 2½ hours | Makes about 7 cups

- ¾ cup sugar
- 3 tablespoons flour
- 1½ teaspoons cinnamon (optional)
- 5 large baking apples, pared,
- cored, and diced into ¾-inch pieces
- Half a stick butter, melted
- 3 tablespoons water
- Nonstick cooking spray

1. Spray interior of crock pot with nonstick cooking spray. 2. In a large bowl, mix sugar and flour together, along with cinnamon if you wish. Set aside. 3. Mix apples, butter, and water together in crock pot. Gently stir in flour mixture until apples are well coated. 4. Cover and cook on high 1½ hours, and then on low 30 to 60 minutes, or until apples are done to your liking. 5. Serve.

Peach-Pecan Grunt

Prep time: 25 minutes | Cook time: 3 hours | Serves 6 to 8

- 4 pounds (1.8 kg) firm but ripe peaches, peeled, halved, pitted, and cut into ½-inch wedges
- 1¾ cups granulated sugar
- 1 tablespoon cornstarch
- 1½ cups all-purpose flour
- 1½ teaspoons baking powder
- ½ teaspoon coarse salt
- ¼ teaspoon ground nutmeg
- ½ cup plus 6 tablespoons (1¾ sticks) unsalted butter, room temperature
- 2 teaspoon vanilla extract
- 2 large eggs
- ½ cup milk
- 1 cup pecans, coarsely chopped
- ¼ cup packed light brown sugar
- Unsweetened whipped cream, for serving

1. Begin by preheating a 5- to 6-quart crock pot. In the pot, combine the peaches with 1 cup of granulated sugar and cornstarch, mixing well. 2. In a separate bowl, whisk together the flour, baking powder, salt, and nutmeg. Using an electric mixer on medium speed, beat ¾ cup (12 tablespoons) of butter with the remaining ¾ cup of granulated sugar and vanilla extract until the mixture is pale and fluffy, which should take about 3 to 5 minutes. Gradually add the eggs, beating in one at a time until fully incorporated. Then, add the flour mixture in three parts, alternating with the milk, mixing until just combined. 3. Spoon the batter evenly over the peaches in the crock pot, smoothing the top with an offset spatula. To prevent condensation, tightly wrap the slow-cooker lid with a clean kitchen towel, gathering the ends at the top. Cover the pot and cook on high until the grunt is firm and the juices are bubbling, which should take about 3 hours, or on low for 6 hours. 4. In a skillet over medium heat, melt the remaining 2 tablespoons of butter. Add the pecans and cook, stirring frequently, until they are lightly toasted, about 5 minutes. Then, stir in the brown sugar and cook for an additional minute, stirring until melted. Immediately transfer the mixture to a plate to cool and break into pieces. Serve the grunt warm, topped with whipped cream and the toasted pecans. Enjoy your delicious dessert!

Decadent Hot Fudge Cake

Prep time: 20 minutes | Cook time: 2 hours | Serves 4 to 6

- ½ cup milk
- 3 tablespoons unsalted butter, melted
- 1 teaspoon vanilla bean paste
- 1 cup granulated sugar
- 1 cup all-purpose flour
- ½ cup cocoa powder (make sure to use natural cocoa
- powder and not Dutch process)
- 2 teaspoons baking powder
- ¾ cup firmly packed light brown sugar
- 1¾ cups boiling water
- Vanilla ice cream or unsweetened whipped cream for serving

1. Coat the insert of a 5- to 7-quart crock pot with nonstick cooking spray. Stir together the milk, butter, and vanilla bean paste in a mixing bowl. Gradually stir in the granulated sugar, flour, ¼ cup of the cocoa powder, and the baking powder. Spread the batter in the prepared slow-cooker insert. 2. Mix together the brown sugar and remaining ¼ cup cocoa powder in a small bowl and sprinkle evenly over the batter. Pour in the boiling water (do not stir). Cover and cook on high for 2 hours, until a skewer inserted into the center comes out clean. Uncover and allow to cool for about 20 minutes. 3. Serve in bowls with vanilla ice cream.

Healthy Cinnamon Apple Delight

Prep time: 15 minutes | Cook time: 2½ to 3 hours | Serves 8

- 1 cup flour
- ¾ cup sugar
- 2 teaspoons baking powder
- 1 teaspoon ground cinnamon
- ¼ teaspoon salt
- 4 medium cooking apples, chopped
- ⅓ cup eggbeaters
- 2 teaspoons vanilla

1. Combine flour, sugar, baking powder, cinnamon, and salt. 2. Add apples, stirring lightly to coat. 3. Combine eggbeaters and vanilla. Add to apple mixture. Stir until just moistened. Spoon into lightly greased crock pot. 4. Cover. Cook on high 2½ to 3 hours. 5. Serve warm.

Maple Cinnamon Crème Brûlée

Prep time: 20 minutes | Cook time: 2 hours | Serves 3

- 1⅓ cups heavy whipping cream
- 3 egg yolks
- ½ cup packed brown sugar
- ¼ teaspoon ground
- cinnamon
- ½ teaspoon maple flavoring
- Topping:
- 1½ teaspoons sugar
- 1½ teaspoons brown sugar

1. In a small saucepan, heat cream until bubbles form around sides of pan. In a small bowl, whisk the egg yolks, brown sugar and cinnamon. Remove cream from the heat; stir a small amount of hot cream into egg mixture. Return all to the pan, stirring constantly. Stir in maple flavoring. 2. Transfer to three 6-oz. ramekins or custard cups. Place in a 6-quart crock pot; add 1 inch of boiling water to crock pot. Cover and cook on high for 2 to 2½ hours or until centers are just set (mixture will jiggle). Carefully remove ramekins from crock pot; cool for 10 minutes. Cover and refrigerate for at least 4 hours. 3. For topping, combine sugar and brown sugar. If using a creme brulee torch, sprinkle custards with sugar mixture. Heat sugar with the torch until caramelized. Serve immediately. 4. If broiling the custards, place ramekins on a baking sheet; let stand at room temperature for 15 minutes. Sprinkle with sugar mixture. Broil 8 inch from the heat for 3 to 5 minutes or until sugar is caramelized. Refrigerate for 1 to 2 hours or until firm.

Piña Colada Bread Pudding

Prep time: 15 minutes | Cook time: 3 hours | Serves 6 to 8

- 8 cups torn stale Hawaiian sweet egg bread, challah, or croissants
- 2 cups ½-inch chunks fresh pineapple
- 1 cup chopped macadamia nuts
- 1½ cups shredded
- sweetened coconut
- 3 cups heavy cream
- 8 large eggs
- 1 tablespoon vanilla extract or bean paste
- ¼ cup dark rum
- 1½ cups sugar

1. Begin by spraying the insert of a 5- to 7-quart crock pot with nonstick cooking spray, or line it with a slow-cooker liner as per the manufacturer's instructions. 2. Place the bread into the slow-cooker insert, then add the pineapple, nuts, and coconut, tossing everything together until well combined. In a large mixing bowl, whisk together the cream, eggs, vanilla, rum, and sugar until fully blended. Pour this mixture over the bread, gently pressing the bread down to ensure it is submerged. 3. Cover the crock pot and cook on high for approximately 3 hours, or until the pudding is puffed and

an instant-read thermometer inserted into the center reads 185°F (85°C). Once done, uncover and let it cool for 30 minutes. 4. Serve the dish warm directly from the cooker for a delightful treat. Enjoy!

Rum Raisin Arborio Pudding

Prep time: 10 minutes | Cook time: 4 hours | Serves 6

- ½ cup raisins
- ¼ cup dark rum
- 1 (12-ounce / 340-g) can evaporated milk
- 1½ cups water
- ⅓ cup granulated sugar
- ¾ cup Arborio rice
- ¼ teaspoon salt
- ¼ teaspoon ground nutmeg

1. In a small bowl, combine the raisins and rum, cover, and set aside to allow the flavors to meld. 2. In a heavy medium saucepan, mix the evaporated milk with 1½ cups of water and bring it to a simmer over medium heat. Once simmering, add the sugar and stir until it dissolves completely. Remove the saucepan from the heat. 3. Pour the milk mixture into the crock pot and stir in the rice and salt until well combined. 4. Cover the crock pot and cook on low for 4 hours, making sure to stir after 1 hour and again after 3 hours. The pudding is ready when it is just set in the center. 5. Drain the raisins and fold them into the pudding along with the nutmeg. Let the pudding stand, uncovered, for 10 minutes. Serve warm, or chill in dessert cups in the fridge for about 3 hours for a refreshing treat. Enjoy!

Cherry Cobbler

Prep time: 10 minutes | Cook time: 2½ to 5½ hours | Serves 6 to 8

- 1 (21-ounce / 595-g) can cherry pie filling
- 1¾ cups dry cake mix of your choice
- 1 egg
- 3 tablespoons evaporated milk
- ½ teaspoon cinnamon
- Nonstick cooking spray

1. Begin by lightly spraying the insert of the crock pot with nonstick cooking spray to prevent sticking. 2. Pour the pie filling into the crock pot and set it to cook on high for 30 minutes to heat through. 3. In the meantime, combine the remaining ingredients in a bowl and mix until the mixture is crumbly. Once the pie filling is hot, spoon the crumbly mixture over the top. 4. Cover the crock pot and cook on low for 2 to 5 hours, or until a toothpick inserted into the center of the topping comes out clean and dry. 5. Once ready, serve the dessert warm or allow it to cool before serving. Enjoy your delicious creation!

Ginger-Spiced Pumpkin Pudding

Prep time: 5 minutes | Cook time: 3 to 4 hours | Serves 8

- 1 tablespoon coconut oil
- 2 cups pumpkin purée
- 1½ cups coconut milk
- 2 eggs
- ½ cup almond flour
- 1 ounce (28 g) protein powder
- 1 tablespoon grated fresh ginger
- ¾ teaspoon liquid stevia
- Pinch ground cloves
- 1 cup whipped coconut cream

1. Lightly grease the insert of the crock pot with coconut oil. 2. In a large bowl, stir together pumpkin, coconut milk, eggs, almond flour, protein powder, ginger, liquid stevia, and cloves. 3. Transfer the mixture to the insert. 4. Cover and cook on low 3 to 4 hours. 5. Serve warm with whipped coconut cream.

Peanut Butter Chocolate Delight Cake

Prep time: 10 minutes | Cook time: 2 to 2½ hours | Serves 8 to 10

- 2 cups dry milk chocolate cake mix
- ½ cup water
- 6 tablespoons peanut butter
- 2 eggs
- ½ cup chopped nuts

1. Combine all ingredients in electric mixer bowl. Beat for 2 minutes. 2. Spray interior of a baking insert, designed to fit into your crock pot. Flour interior of greased insert. Pour batter into insert. Place insert in crock pot. 3. Cover insert with 8 paper towels. 4. Cover cooker. Cook on high 2 to 2½ hours, or until toothpick inserted into center of cake comes out clean. 5. Allow cake to cool. Then invert onto a serving plate, cut, and serve.

Stewed Apricots

Prep time: 10 minutes | Cook time: 2 to 4 hours | Serves 6 to 8

- 1⅓ pounds (605 g) dried apricots, pitted
- 1 teaspoon ground cinnamon
- 1 cup granulated sugar
- 1 to 1¼ cups water
- ⅓ cup heavy cream
- 2 tablespoons toasted almond slivers

1. Set the crock pot to high and add the apricots, cinnamon, sugar, and water, stirring to combine. 2. Cover the pot and cook on high for 2 hours, or on low for 4 hours, until the apricots are tender. 3. Once cooked, transfer the mixture to a large bowl and let it cool before chilling it in the refrigerator. 4. Just before serving, whip the cream until it reaches your desired consistency. Serve the chilled apricot mixture in individual glasses, topped with whipped cream and a sprinkle of nuts for added texture and flavor. Enjoy your delicious dessert!

Rice Pudding

Prep time: 10 minutes | Cook time: 5 hours | Serves 2

- Nonstick cooking spray
- 1 cup short-grain white rice
- 5 cups milk
- 1 cup light cream
- ½ cup chopped peeled kiwi
- ½ cup sugar
- 1 tablespoon butter
- 2 teaspoons vanilla
- ½ cup chopped mango

1. Start by spraying the insert of the crock pot with nonstick cooking spray to prevent sticking. 2. In the crock pot, mix all the ingredients together except for the mango and kiwi, stirring well to combine. 3. Cover the crock pot and set it to cook on low for 5 hours, or until the rice is tender and the pudding has thickened. If you're at home, give it a stir a few times during cooking to ensure even texture. 4. Once cooked, top the pudding with the diced mango and kiwi, then serve warm. Enjoy your delightful dish!

Amaretto-Braised Pears with Crunchy Almond Topping

Prep time: 15 minutes | Cook time: 4 hours | Serves 6 to 8

- ½ cup amaretto liqueur
- 1 cup pear nectar
- 1½ cups firmly packed light brown sugar
- ½ cup (1 stick) unsalted butter, melted
- 6 firm red pears, peeled and cored
- ½ cup crushed amaretti cookies (about 6)
- ½ cup chopped almonds, toasted

1. Combine the amaretto, nectar, sugar, and butter in the insert of a 5- to 7-quart crock pot and stir until the sugar is dissolved. Stand the pears in the liquid, stem-ends up. Cover and cook on low for 4 hours until the pears are tender. 2. Combine the cookie crumbs and almonds in a small bowl and set aside. Uncover the pears and allow to cool. 3. Serve each pear in a pool of the sauce and sprinkled with some of the almond mixture.

Cinnamon-Spiced Stuffed Apples with Fig and Walnut Filling

Prep time: 10 minutes | Cook time: 2 to 5 hours | Serves 4

- 4 medium-sized tart cooking apples (like Granny Smith or Braeburn)
- ⅓ cup finely chopped dried figs or raisins
- ½ cup finely chopped walnuts
- ¼ cup packed light brown sugar
- ½ teaspoon apple pie spice or cinnamon
- ¼ cup apple juice
- 1 tablespoon butter, cut into 4 pieces

1. Core the apples. Cut a strip of peel from the top of each apple. Place the apples upright in the crock pot. 2. In a small bowl, combine figs, walnuts, brown sugar, and apple pie spice. Spoon the mixture into the center of the apples, patting in with a knife or a narrow metal spatula. 3. Pour the apple juice around the apples in the crock pot. 4. Top each apple with a piece of butter. 5. Cover and cook on low for 4 to 5 hours or on high for 2 to 2½ hours until very tender. 6. Serve warm, with some of the cooking liquid spooned over the apples.

Tropical Coconut Macadamia Bread Pudding

Prep time: 25 minutes | Cook time: 4½ hours | Serves 8 to 10

- 8 cups 1-inch cubes or torn stale sturdy white bread, such as Pepperidge Farm
- 1½ cups shredded sweetened coconut
- 1 cup chopped macadamia nuts
- 1½ cups milk-chocolate chips, such as Ghirardelli or Guittard
- 1 (13- to 14-ounce / 369- to 397-g) can coconut milk
- 1 cup milk
- 1 cup heavy cream
- 8 large eggs
- ½ cup firmly packed light brown sugar
- ¼ cup dark rum (optional)
- Hot fudge, berry, or buttered rum sauce for serving

1. Coat the insert of a 5- to 7-quart crock pot with nonstick cooking spray. Put the bread, coconut, macadamia nuts, and chocolate chips in a large bowl. In another bowl, whisk together the coconut milk, milk, cream, eggs, sugar, and rum (if using). 2. Pour the milk mixture over the bread and stir until the bread is soaked. Transfer the bread mixture to the slow-cooker insert. Cover and cook on low for 4 hours, until the pudding is cooked through and an instant-read thermometer inserted in the center reads 170°F (77°C). Uncover and cook for an additional 30 minutes. 3. Serve the pudding with hot fudge sauce, berry sauce, or buttered rum sauce.

Crock-Baked Apples

Prep time: 15 minutes | Cook time: 2½ to 3 hours | Serves 8

- 8 medium apples
- ½ cup golden raisins
- ½ cup finely chopped walnuts
- 1 cup firmly packed light brown sugar
- 1 teaspoon ground cinnamon
- 2 tablespoons dark rum
- 4 tablespoons (½ stick) unsalted butter, melted and slightly cooled
- 1½ cups apple juice or apple cider
- Unsweetened whipped cream, for garnish
- Cinnamon sugar, for garnish

1. Begin by coring the apples and placing them in the insert of a 5- to 7-quart crock pot. In a mixing bowl, combine the raisins, walnuts, sugar, cinnamon, rum, and butter, stirring until well blended. Stuff the mixture into the hollowed apples. Pour apple juice into the bottom of the crock pot insert. Cover the pot and cook on low for 2½ to 3 hours, or on high until the apples are tender. 2. Once cooked, carefully remove the apples using a spatula to catch any filling that may fall out. 3. Serve the stuffed apples warm, drizzled with the sauce from the bottom of the crock pot, and add a dollop of whipped cream topped with a sprinkle of cinnamon sugar. Enjoy your delightful dessert!

Maple Pumpkin Bread Pudding Delight

Prep time: 10 minutes | Cook time: 3½ hours | Serves 8

- 1½ cups heavy cream
- 1 (16-ounce / 454-g) can pumpkin purée (2 cups)
- 4 large eggs
- ½ cup maple syrup
- ½ cup firmly packed light brown sugar
- 2 teaspoons ground cinnamon
- ¼ teaspoon ground cloves
- ¼ teaspoon freshly grated nutmeg
- ⅛ teaspoon ground ginger
- 9 cups torn egg bread or leftover croissants

1. Coat the insert of a 5- to 7-quart crock pot with nonstick cooking spray or line with a slow-cooker liner according to the manufacturer's directions. 2. Whisk all the ingredients except the bread in a large mixing bowl until smooth. Add the bread to the bowl and stir to soak the bread. Transfer the mixture to the slow-cooker insert. Cover and cook on high for about 3½ hours, until puffed and an instant-read thermometer registers 185°F (85°C). Allow the pudding to rest for about 30 minutes. 3. Serve from the cooker set on warm.

Crock Pot Apple Pudding Cake

Prep time: 15 minutes | Cook time: 2 hours | Serves 10

- 2 cups all-purpose flour
- ⅔ cup plus ¼ cup sugar, divided
- 3 teaspoons baking powder
- 1 teaspoon salt
- ½ cup cold butter
- 1 cup 2% milk
- 2 medium tart apples, peeled and chopped
- 1½ cups orange juice
- ½ cup honey
- 2 tablespoons butter, melted
- 1 teaspoon ground cinnamon
- 1⅓ cups sour cream
- ¼ cup confectioners' sugar

1. In a small bowl, mix together the flour, ⅔ cup sugar, baking powder, and salt. Cut in the butter until the mixture resembles coarse crumbs. Stir in the milk just until the batter is moistened. Spread this mixture into the bottom of a greased 4- or 5-quart crock pot, then sprinkle the apple slices evenly over the batter. 2. In another small bowl, whisk together the orange juice, honey, melted butter, cinnamon, and the remaining sugar. Pour this mixture over the apples in the crock pot. Cover and cook on high for 2 to 3 hours, or until the apples are tender and the pudding cake is set. 3. In a separate small bowl, mix the sour cream with confectioners' sugar until smooth. Serve this sweet topping alongside the warm pudding cake for a delightful treat. Enjoy!

Carrot Cake

Prep time: 15 minutes | Cook time: 3 hours | Serves 8

- ½ cup coconut oil, melted, divided
- 1 cup granulated erythritol
- 2 eggs
- ¼ cup almond milk
- 2 teaspoons pure vanilla extract
- 1½ cups almond flour
- 1 teaspoon baking powder
- 1 teaspoon ground cinnamon
- ½ teaspoon baking soda
- ½ teaspoon ground ginger
- ¼ teaspoon ground nutmeg
- Pinch ground allspice
- 1 cup finely shredded carrots

1. Start by lightly greasing a 7-inch springform pan with 1 tablespoon of coconut oil to prevent sticking. 2. In a large bowl, use a handheld mixer to combine the remaining coconut oil, erythritol, eggs, almond milk, and vanilla extract until the mixture is well blended. 3. In a medium bowl, mix together the almond flour, baking powder, cinnamon, baking soda, ginger, nutmeg, and allspice until evenly combined. 4. Gradually add the dry ingredients to the wet ingredients, stirring until just combined. 5. Fold in the grated carrots until they are uniformly mixed throughout the batter. 6. Pour the batter into the prepared springform pan, smoothing the top with a spatula for an even surface. 7. Place a wire rack in the insert of the crock pot and set the springform pan on top of the rack. 8. Cover the crock pot and cook on low for 3 hours, or until a toothpick inserted into the center of the cake comes out clean. 9. Once cooked, allow the cake to cool before serving. Enjoy your delicious carrot cake!

Port–Infused Figs with Blue Cheese and Walnuts

Prep time: 10 minutes | Cook time: 1½ to 2 hours | Serves 6

- 1½ cups Ruby Port
- 1 cup firmly packed light brown sugar
- 2 whole cloves
- 12 fresh figs
- 1½ cups crumbled Point Reyes blue cheese
- 1 cup chopped toasted walnuts

1. Combine the port, sugar, and cloves in the insert of a 5- to 7-quart crock pot. Add the figs stem-end up to the slow-cooker insert and spoon some of the syrup over the figs. Cover and cook on low for 1½ to 2 hours. Allow the figs to cool in the syrup for 1 hour. 2. Remove the figs to a serving platter. Strain the syrup through a fine-mesh sieve into a saucepan and boil for 5 to 10 minutes until it is thickened. Allow the syrup to cool slightly. 3. Arrange 2 figs in a pool of the syrup on each plate. Sprinkle with the crumbled blue cheese and toasted walnuts before serving.

Decadent Double Chocolate Bread Pudding

Prep time: 25 minutes | Cook time: 3 hours | Serves 2

- Nonstick cooking spray
- 6 cups cubed French bread
- 1 cup semisweet chocolate chips
- 2 cups chocolate milk
- 4 eggs, beaten
- 3 tablespoons butter, melted
- ½ cup brown sugar
- ¼ cup granulated sugar
- 3 tablespoons cocoa powder
- 2 teaspoons vanilla

1. Line the crock pot with heavy-duty foil, and spray with the nonstick cooking spray. 2. In the crock pot, combine the French bread and chocolate chips. 3. In a large bowl, beat all the remaining ingredients. Pour the mixture into the crock pot. 4. Push the bread under the liquid. Let stand for 20 minutes. 5. Cover and cook on low for 3 hours, or until the mixture is set and reads 160°F (71°C) on a food thermometer, and serve.

Cardamom-Infused Pakistani Sweet Rice with Nutty Toppings

- 2 cups basmati rice
- 4 tablespoons butter or ghee
- 4 cups hot water
- 1 large pinch saffron, crushed and mixed with 2 tablespoons hot water, or a yellow food coloring
- 6 green cardamom pods
- ¾ to 1 cup sugar
- 2 tablespoons crushed unsalted pistachios
- 2 tablespoons slivered almonds

1. Wash the rice in a few changes of water until it runs clear, and then soak it in warm water for 10 minutes. 2. Rub a little of the butter or ghee on the inside of your crock pot and turn it to high. Drain the washed rice and place it in the crock pot. Add the hot water and saffron water (or the food coloring). Stir to mix. This should color the rice, giving it the bright yellow it's famous for. 3. Cover and cook for 2 hours on high. Stir the rice halfway through the cooking time. When cooked, remove the rice and set it aside in a colander. 4. Turn the cooker to high and add the rest of the butter to melt, then crack in the cardamom pods. Stir in the sugar and 4 tablespoons of water (add a little more if required). Stir to melt the sugar. 5. Cook gently for about 5 minutes to produce a syrup. Add most of the nuts, reserving some for a garnish. 6. Gently stir the rice back into the cooker and fold it, so that each grain is coated with the sugar syrup. 7. Cover and turn the cooker to low. Cook for another 5 to 10 minutes. 8. Serve warm, topped with the remaining nuts.

Apple-Pear Streusel

- Nonstick cooking spray
- 4 apples, peeled and sliced
- 2 pears, peeled and sliced
- ¼ cup brown sugar
- 1 tablespoon freshly squeezed lemon juice
- ½ teaspoon ground cinnamon
- 2 tablespoons butter, plus 3 tablespoons cut into cubes, divided
- ½ cup light cream
- 1 cup all-purpose flour
- ½ cup rolled oats
- ½ cup chopped pecans
- ⅓ cup granulated sugar

1. Begin by spraying the insert of the crock pot with nonstick cooking spray to prevent sticking. 2. In the crock pot, combine the apple and pear slices, then sprinkle them with brown sugar, lemon juice, and cinnamon, mixing everything together. Dot the mixture with 2 tablespoons of butter and pour the cream evenly over the top. 3. In a medium bowl, mix together the flour, oats, pecans, and granulated sugar. Add the remaining 3 tablespoons of butter in cubes, and use two knives or a pastry blender to cut the butter in until the mixture is crumbly. 4. Evenly sprinkle the crumbly mixture over the fruit in the crock pot. 5. Cover the crock pot and cook on low for 7 hours, or until the fruit is tender and the flavors meld beautifully. Enjoy your delicious dessert!

Crunchy Peanut Butter Candy Clusters

- 2 pounds (907 g) white candy coating, coarsely chopped
- 1½ cups peanut butter
- ½ teaspoon almond extract
- (optional)
- 4 cups Cap'n Crunch cereal
- 4 cups crisp rice cereal
- 4 cups miniature marshmallows

1. Place candy coating in a 5-quart crock pot. Cover and cook on high for 1 hour. Add peanut butter. Stir in extract if desired. 2. In a large bowl, combine the cereals and marshmallows. Stir in the peanut butter mixture until well coated. Drop by tablespoonfuls onto waxed paper. Let stand until set. Store at room temperature.

Caramel Apples

- 4 very large tart apples, cored
- ½ cup apple juice
- 8 tablespoons brown sugar
- 12 hot cinnamon candies
- 4 tablespoons butter
- 8 caramel candies
- ¼ teaspoon ground cinnamon
- Whipped cream

1. Start by removing a ½-inch-wide strip of peel from the top of each apple, then place the apples in the crock pot. 2. Pour apple juice evenly over the apples to help them cook. 3. In the center of each apple, fill with 2 tablespoons of brown sugar, 3 hot cinnamon candies, 1 tablespoon of butter, and 2 caramel candies. Sprinkle the tops with a dash of cinnamon for added flavor. 4. Cover the crock pot and cook on low for 4 to 6 hours, or until the apples are tender and cooked through. 5. Once ready, serve the apples hot, topped with whipped cream for a delightful treat. Enjoy!

Blueberry Crisp

- 5 tablespoons coconut oil, melted, divided
- 4 cups blueberries
- ¾ cup plus 2 tablespoons granulated erythritol
- 1 cup ground pecans

- 1 teaspoon baking soda
- ½ teaspoon ground cinnamon
- 2 tablespoons coconut milk
- 1 egg

1. Begin by lightly greasing the insert of a 4-quart crock pot with 1 tablespoon of coconut oil to prevent sticking. 2. Add the blueberries along with 2 tablespoons of erythritol to the crock pot insert. 3. In a large mixing bowl, combine the remaining ¾ cup of erythritol, ground pecans, baking soda, and cinnamon, stirring until everything is well blended. 4. Incorporate the coconut milk, egg, and the remaining coconut oil into the dry mixture, stirring until it forms coarse crumbs. 5. Spoon the pecan mixture over the blueberries in the crock pot, spreading it evenly on top. 6. Cover the crock pot and cook on low for 3 to 4 hours, allowing the flavors to meld together. 7. Once finished, serve the dish warm and enjoy your delicious dessert!

Decadent Chocolate Croissant Pudding

- 8 cups torn stale croissants, egg bread, or challah
- 3 cups chopped bittersweet or semisweet chocolate
- 4 tablespoons (½ stick) unsalted butter, melted
- 3 cups heavy cream

- 8 large eggs
- 1 tablespoon vanilla bean paste or extract
- 1 cup sugar

1. Coat the insert of a 5- to 7-quart crock pot with nonstick cooking spray or line it with a slow-cooker liner according to the manufacturer's directions. 2. Arrange the bread in the crock pot and sprinkle with 1½ cups of the chocolate. Melt the remaining chocolate with the butter in a small saucepan over low heat. Remove from the heat and allow to cool. 3. Whisk together the melted chocolate, cream, eggs, vanilla bean paste, and sugar in a large mixing bowl until blended; the mixture may look curdled. Pour over the bread and chocolate and push the bread down to submerge it. 4. Cover and cook on high for about 3 hours, until puffed and an instant-read meat thermometer inserted in the center registers 185°F (85°C). Uncover and allow to cool for 30 minutes. 5. Serve in the cooker set on warm.

Chapter 10
Pizzas, Wraps, and Sandwiches

Chapter 10 Pizzas, Wraps, and Sandwiches

Savory Sloppy Joes with a Tangy Twist

Prep time: 15 minutes | Cook time: 3 to 10 hours | Makes 12 sandwiches

- 3 pounds (1.4 kg) ground beef, browned and drained
- 1 onion, finely chopped
- 1 green pepper, chopped
- 2 (8-ounce / 227-g) cans tomato sauce
- ¾ cup ketchup
- 1 tablespoon Worcestershire sauce
- 1 teaspoon chili powder
- ¼ teaspoon pepper
- ¼ teaspoon garlic powder
- Rolls, for serving

1. Combine all ingredients except rolls in crock pot. 2. Cover. Cook on low 8 to 10 hours, or on high 3 to 4 hours. 3. Serve.

Enchilada Pie

Prep time: 40 minutes | Cook time: 4 hours | Serves 8

- 1 (12-ounce / 340-g) package frozen vegetarian meat crumbles
- 1 cup chopped onion
- ½ cup chopped green pepper
- 2 teaspoons canola oil
- 1 (16-ounce / 454-g) can kidney beans, rinsed and drained
- 1 (15-ounce / 425-g) can black beans, rinsed and
- drained
- 1 (10-ounce / 283-g) can diced tomatoes and green chilies, undrained
- ½ cup water
- 1½ teaspoons chili powder
- ½ teaspoon ground cumin
- ¼ teaspoon pepper
- 6 whole wheat tortillas
- 2 cups shredded reduced-fat cheddar cheese

1. Start by cutting three strips of heavy-duty foil, each measuring 25x3 inches. Arrange them in a crisscross pattern at the bottom of a 5-quart crock pot so they resemble spokes of a wheel. Ensure the strips extend up the sides of the pot and coat them with cooking spray to prevent sticking. 2. In a large saucepan, heat oil over medium heat and cook the meat crumbles, onion, and green pepper until the vegetables are tender. Stir in both cans of beans, tomatoes, water, chili powder, cumin, and pepper. Bring the mixture to a boil, then reduce the heat and let it simmer uncovered for 10 minutes. 3. In the prepared crock pot, layer about 1 cup of the bean mixture, followed by a tortilla and ⅓ cup of cheese. Repeat these layers five times, ensuring even distribution. Cover the pot and cook on low for 4 to 5 hours, or until everything is heated through and the cheese is melted. 4. Once cooked, use the foil strips as handles to carefully lift the pie out of the crock pot and transfer it to a platter for serving. Enjoy your delicious dish!

Beef and Veggie Sloppy Joes

Prep time: 35 minutes | Cook time: 5 hours | Serves 12

- 4 medium carrots, shredded (about 3½ cups)
- 1 medium yellow summer squash, shredded (about 2 cups)
- 1 medium zucchini, shredded (about 2 cups)
- 1 medium sweet red pepper, finely chopped
- 2 medium tomatoes, seeded and chopped
- 1 small red onion, finely chopped
- ½ cup ketchup
- 3 tablespoons minced fresh basil or 3 teaspoons dried basil
- 3 tablespoons molasses
- 2 tablespoons cider vinegar
- 2 garlic cloves, minced
- ½ teaspoon salt
- ½ teaspoon pepper
- 2 pounds (907 g) lean ground beef (90% lean)
- 12 whole wheat hamburger buns, split

1. In a 5- or 6-quart crock pot, combine the first 13 ingredients, mixing them well to ensure even distribution. In a large skillet over medium heat, cook the beef for 8 to 10 minutes, breaking it into crumbles, until it is no longer pink. Drain any excess fat, then transfer the cooked beef to the crock pot. Stir everything together until well combined. 2. Cover the crock pot and cook on low for 5 to 6 hours, or until the mixture is heated through and the vegetables are tender. Once ready, use a slotted spoon to serve the beef mixture on buns for a delicious meal. Enjoy!

Beach Boy's Pot Roast

Prep time: 10 minutes | Cook time: 8 to 12 hours | Makes 6 to 8 sandwiches

- 1 (3- to 4-pound / 1.4- to 1.8-kg) chuck or top round roast
- 8 to 12 slivers of garlic
- 1 (32-ounce / 907-g) jar
- pepperoncini peppers, undrained
- 6 to 8 large hoagie rolls
- 12 to 16 slices of your favorite cheese

1. Begin by making slits in the roast using a sharp knife and inserting slivers of garlic into each slit for added flavor. 2. Place the seasoned beef in the crock pot, then spoon the peppers along with all of their juice over the top of the roast. 3. Cover the crock pot and set it to cook on low for 8 to 12 hours, or until the meat is tender but not dry. 4. Once the cooking time is complete, carefully remove the meat from the cooker and let it cool slightly. Then, use two forks to shred the beef into bite-sized pieces. 5. Serve the shredded beef on hoagie rolls and top with cheese for a delicious sandwich. Enjoy your meal!

Herbed Beef Sandwiches with Savory Onion Soup Gravy

Prep time: 5 minutes | Cook time: 7 to 8 hours | Makes 10 to 12 sandwiches

- 1 (3- to 4-pound / 1.4- to 1.8-kg) boneless beef chuck roast
- 3 tablespoons fresh basil, or 1 tablespoon dried basil
- 3 tablespoons fresh oregano, or 1 tablespoon dried oregano
- 1½ cups water
- 1 package dry onion soup mix
- 10 to 12 Italian rolls

1. Place roast in crock pot. 2. Combine basil, oregano, and water. Pour over roast. 3. Sprinkle with onion soup mix. 4. Cover. Cook on low 7 to 8 hours. Shred meat with fork. 5. Serve on Italian rolls.

Zesty French Sandwiches

Prep time: 5 minutes | Cook time: 8 hours | Makes 6 to 8 sandwiches

- 1 (4-pound / 1.8-kg) beef roast
- 1 (10½-ounce / 298-g) can beef broth
- 1 (10½-ounce / 298-g) can condensed French onion
- soup
- 1 (12-ounce / 340-g) bottle of beer
- 6 to 8 French rolls or baguettes

1. Start by patting the roast dry and placing it in the crock pot. 2. In a mixing bowl, combine the beef broth, onion soup, and beer until well blended, then pour this mixture over the meat in the crock pot. 3. Cover the pot and cook on low for 8 hours, or until the meat is tender yet not dry. 4. While the meat is cooking, split the rolls or baguettes and warm them in the oven or microwave until heated through. 5. Once the cooking time is complete, carefully remove the meat from the cooker and let it rest for 10 minutes. After resting, shred the meat with two forks or slice it diagonally into thin pieces, and place it inside the warmed rolls. Serve and enjoy your delicious meal!

Savory Sausage and Pepper Hoagies

Prep time: 15 minutes | Cook time: 6 hours | Serves 6

- 6 Italian sausage link
- 1 medium green pepper, cut into 1-inch pieces
- 1 large onion, cut into 1-inch pieces
- 1 (8-ounce / 227-g) can tomato sauce
- ⅛ teaspoon pepper
- 6 hoagie or submarine sandwich buns, split

1. In a large skillet, brown sausage links over medium heat. Cut into ½-inch slices; place in a 3-quart crock pot. Stir in the green pepper, onion, tomato sauce and pepper. 2. Cover and cook on low for 6 to 8 hours or until sausage is no longer pink and vegetables are tender. Use a slotted spoon to serve on buns.

Herby French Sandwiches

Prep time: 5 minutes | Cook time: 5 to 6 hours | Makes 6 to 8 sandwiches

- 1 (3-pound / 1.4-kg) chuck roast
- 2 cups water
- ½ cup soy sauce
- 1 teaspoon garlic powder
- 1 bay leaf
- 3 to 4 whole peppercorns
- 1 teaspoon dried rosemary (optional)
- 1 teaspoon dried thyme (optional)
- 6 to 8 French rolls

1. Begin by placing the roast in the crock pot. 2. In a mixing bowl, combine all remaining ingredients until well mixed, then pour this mixture over the meat in the crock pot. 3. Cover the pot and cook on high for 5 to 6 hours, or until the meat is tender yet not dry. 4. Once cooked, remove the meat from the broth and use a fork to shred it into pieces. Stir the shredded meat back into the sauce for flavor. 5. Using a large fork, scoop out portions of the meat and place them on French rolls for serving. Enjoy your delicious sandwiches!

Tender Shredded Beef Sandwiches with Savory Dipping Broth

Prep time: 10 minutes | Cook time: 8 to 10 hours | Makes 10 sandwiches

- 3 pounds (1.4 kg) beef chuck roast
- 1 large onion, chopped
- ¼ cup vinegar
- 1 clove garlic, minced

- 1 to 1½ teaspoons salt
- ¼ to ½ teaspoon pepper
- Hamburger buns, for serving

1. Place meat in crock pot. Top with onions. 2. Combine vinegar, garlic, salt, and pepper. Pour over meat. 3. Cover. Cook on low 8 to 10 hours. 4. Drain broth but save for dipping. 5. Shred meat. 6. Serve on hamburger buns with broth on side.

Italian Turkey Sloppy Joes

Prep time: 15 minutes | Cook time: 3 to 4 hours | Makes 12 sandwiches

- 1½ pounds (680 g) ground turkey, browned in nonstick skillet
- 1 cup chopped onions
- 2 cups low-sodium tomato sauce
- 1 cup fresh mushrooms, sliced

- 2 tablespoons Splenda
- 1 to 2 tablespoons Italian seasoning, according to your taste preference
- 12 reduced-calorie hamburger buns
- 12 slices low-fat Mozzarella cheese (optional)

1. Place ground turkey, onions, tomato sauce, and mushrooms in crock pot. 2. Stir in Splenda and Italian seasoning. 3. Cover. Cook on low 3 to 4 hours. 4. Serve ¼ cup of Sloppy Joe mixture on each bun, topped with cheese, if desired.

Appendix 1: Measurement Conversion Chart

VOLUME EQUIVALENTS(DRY)

US STANDARD	METRIC (APPROXIMATE)
1/8 teaspoon	0.5 mL
1/4 teaspoon	1 mL
1/2 teaspoon	2 mL
3/4 teaspoon	4 mL
1 teaspoon	5 mL
1 tablespoon	15 mL
1/4 cup	59 mL
1/2 cup	118 mL
3/4 cup	177 mL
1 cup	235 mL
2 cups	475 mL
3 cups	700 mL
4 cups	1 L

VOLUME EQUIVALENTS(LIQUID)

US STANDARD	US STANDARD (OUNCES)	METRIC (APPROXIMATE)
2 tablespoons	1 fl.oz.	30 mL
1/4 cup	2 fl.oz.	60 mL
1/2 cup	4 fl.oz.	120 mL
1 cup	8 fl.oz.	240 mL
1 1/2 cup	12 fl.oz.	355 mL
2 cups or 1 pint	16 fl.oz.	475 mL
4 cups or 1 quart	32 fl.oz.	1 L
1 gallon	128 fl.oz.	4 L

TEMPERATURES EQUIVALENTS

FAHRENHEIT(F)	CELSIUS(C) (APPROXIMATE)
225 °F	107 °C
250 °F	120 °C
275 °F	135 °C
300 °F	150 °C
325 °F	160 °C
350 °F	180 °C
375 °F	190 °C
400 °F	205 °C
425 °F	220 °C
450 °F	235 °C
475 °F	245 °C
500 °F	260 °C

WEIGHT EQUIVALENTS

US STANDARD	METRIC (APPROXIMATE)
1 ounce	28 g
2 ounces	57 g
5 ounces	142 g
10 ounces	284 g
15 ounces	425 g
16 ounces (1 pound)	455 g
1.5 pounds	680 g
2 pounds	907 g

Appendix 2: Recipes Index

Made in the USA
Coppell, TX
25 November 2024

40951141R00059